AN IMAGE
DARKLY FORMING
Women and Initiation

BANI SHORTER

ROUTLEDGE & KEGAN PAUL
LONDON AND NEW YORK

First published in 1987 by
Routledge & Kegan Paul Ltd
11 New Fetter Lane, London EC4P 4EE

Published in the USA by
Routledge & Kegan Paul Inc
in association with Methuen Inc
29 West 35th Street, New York, NY 10001

Set in Palatino
by Inforum Ltd
and printed in Great Britain
by The Guernsey Press Co Ltd
Guernsey, Channel Islands

Library of Congress Cataloging in Publication Data

Shorter, Bani
   An image darkly forming.

   Bibliography p.
   Includes index.
   1. Women—Psychology I Title
HQ1206.S49 1987   155 6'33   86-31542

British Library CIP Data also available
ISBN 0-7102-0574-0

Those who have best prepared me
for the writing of this book
have been men,
but it is dedicated
to five women
and Mary Briner

WOMAN IN LOVE

Yes, I'm longing for you. Self-succumbing,
to outslip my own hand I begin,
with no hope of ever overcoming
what to me, as from your side, is coming,
grave and undeterred and unakin.

. . in those days· I was so undistracted,
untold, undivulged by anything,
like a stone's my silence was protracted
over which a brook runs murmuring

Now, though, in these weeks when Spring has woken,
by a something I've been slowly broken
from the dark unconscious year away.
Through some power my poor warm life is going
into hands of one not even knowing
what I still was only yesterday

Rilke, 'Woman in Love'
first published, 1906

CONTENTS

PREFACE

An analyst does not see cases but people and it is not illnesses which come asking to be healed; it is persons. In therapeutic companionship with five women I was made aware of how they were challenged and changed during crucial periods of transition in their lives, which is the same as to say how they were initiated into being themselves. In the midst of this process they revealed who they were and recognised dimensions of themselves which had formerly been repressed and undreamed of. This is the story of journeys made into depth and what I discovered about the psychology of women and initiation as a consequence. What each of my analysands discovered remains for her to be.

Primarily this is a book for women, about women. It is also a book about the processes of analysis for those in analysis. Hopefully, it will be of equal but different value and meaning both for my analytic colleagues and for those who work with them. It may also be of interest to certain anthropologists or social workers who are likewise called upon to become careful observers of human nature and feel the need to draw conclusions about the inter-relationships of individuals and cultures, persons and groups. It speaks about guidance, guiding and being guided to all who work with psyche or soul.

Because psychological experiences involve people total-ly, there is no area of life that can be excluded from analysis and because initiations are disruptive, these women were bewildered and in search of relevance, the relevance of the part to the whole without which no prac-tice – psychological, medical, educational, religious or otherwise, is either healing or satisfying. By responding to unconscious promptings that resulted in unplanned sym-bolic enactments, I saw these persons realign themselves according to age-old traditions which were integral to the healing of their psychic disabilities and themselves. Alongside them, I was also initiated to live and validated insights. I hope this book will be initiatory of insight for others too.

ACKNOWLEDGMENTS

I acknowledge my gratitude to the Center for Creative Photography, University of Arizona for permission to use the photograph by Edward Weston which appears on the cover of this book This is a photograph of his wife, Charis. It dramatically suggests the process of inward reflection which is essential in the psychological discovery of a woman as herself and this is what I have written about.

Thanks are also extended to the Hogarth Press for permission to reprint the poem entitled 'Woman in Love' published in *The Selected Works*, volume 2, Rainer Maria Rilke, translated by J.B Leishman. Routledge & Kegan Paul have generously allowed me to quote extensively from *The Collected Works* of C.G. Jung.

The substance of the book is drawn from the lives of persons who could not have known what they were contributing at the time. To work with them was a privilege. When the design of what we did became apparent, none of them withdrew, objected, changed or withheld her records. I am grateful.

There have been many friends who, whether consciously or otherwise, have contributed to the book by listening, discussing, criticising, encouraging and making suggestions. Several of the chapters were first given as lectures or used with students: at the New England Society of Jungian Analysts, at the 'Journey Toward Wholeness' conference in Florida (1982), before The Washington Society for Jungian Psychology, Washington D.C., for students in training at the C.G Jung Institute, Zurich, and at a one day conference offered by the Analytical Psychology Club, London. The presentations affirmed the demand of therapists for such material and suggested the interest of persons of both sexes in publication Andrew Samuels, colleague and associate, first saw the shape of a book in the development of the lectures.

Jane Williams and Hilary Hill have typed the manuscript

Prudence Scott and Paul and Martha Lawrence have provided space where I could write, space and time, here and in Ireland Without their generosity it would not have been possible

Bani Shorter

CHAPTER 1

THE NATURE
OF THE EVIDENCE

.   it is the reader's task to perceive the providential design
which has arranged the events in the order in which the work
presents them and with the results which it describes. Yet it is
the design that justifies these events and results and gives
them a meaning.

Dumézil, *The Destiny of a King*

We begin with five women
The first was forty-seven years of age; meagre, thin and spare She dressed in coarse trousers and jackets; her body showed hardly a trace of feminine contour. She was confused and often disturbed. She sometimes had difficulty finding her way to my consulting room. Occasionally neighbours would say, 'That young boy who comes to see you must have arrived at the wrong time. I saw him standing outside this afternoon'; or, 'You weren't here. He tried the bell several times and then went away frowning '

I am a Jungian analyst. Jen and I have now worked together for many years, seeing one another two or three times a week for prolonged periods at the beginning of her analysis and, later, as she has been able to afford it. In the beginning she was strongly hysterical, with a compelling unconscious capacity to convert into bodily symptoms her inability to meet and integrate new experience. So she was often ill, absent from work and absent from analysis.

She was regarded as a misfit anyway, second-rate, unreliable and qualified to be employed only for limited and menial jobs. Jen was an outsider, estranged from most human beings her own age, a comical person and often made fun of Finding a friend in me, someone who listened and paid attention, she clung passionately and controllingly to our relationship. But we didn't live in the same town, or even in the same country. So sometimes she would have to leave for a while until she could come back and see me.

There are many ways to describe or diagnose what was wrong or had gone wrong with Jen. She presented an encyclopaedia of symptoms and a thesaurus of linked causes. But she could also be said to be suffering from a chronic, life-long depression traceable to her being disassociated from awareness of herself as a girl with potential for maturing with the body and mind of a woman. Time had stopped for her at an indeterminate and undefined stage sexually, though not genitally She came to me because her psychic condition was untenable, baffling and uncomfortable. But she could not have voiced how or from what she felt she suffered. It was in the darkness of inarticulate imagery that we groped for an undiscovered and, to her, unrecognisable person.

Certainly she had been rejected by her parents but it is not my purpose here to tell her entire story or to give a detailed case history And, although what I will report became part of an ongoing and more satisfying life for Jen, what happened is not proof of the superiority of one analytic school over another any more than it is suggestive of particular competence on my part. But I want to relate something of what transpired between her and me because of what it told me, stimulating my awareness of what it means to be a woman, person, patient, therapist. Jen and I have learned from one another.

'Clinical' refers to a point of view or perspective toward what can be seen as morbid or pathological, although it is often spoken of as a method. Perhaps this is inevitable since a doctor or therapist will both approach his work and proceed with a case in light of what he perceives to be wrong. In a tradition which has grown out of medicine, the first clinical model for analysis was naturally that of diagnosis and cure Jung's perception that psychic illness pertains to the whole person has necessitated a different clinical approach, however. The application and further clarification of this perspective and technique has been a matter of continuing concern among later generations of depth psychologists and analysts, myself included.

Acceptable or not by today's standards, Jung considered himself a scientist and affirmed the authenticity of his researches. This led certain of his followers to adopt a more structured approach to their work and its interpretations, proceeding on the basis of hypothesis and verification of concepts. Others adopted a wider ranging, less programmed approach, allowing themselves and their patients to be guided to a greater degree by the compensatory symbolism of the unconscious itself. But both groups have applied themselves clinically then and now, i.e in relation to that which is wrong, out of balance, morbid or pathological in the personality, and both approaches have required incisive observation, application, summary and reference to a theoretical framework.

My own view is that working on the borderlines of neurotic and psychotic disturbance, we are involved with nothing less than the total personality. We are inevitably faced with what is wrong but at the same time we must consider how that pathology relates to the healthy individual and to the end toward which his recovery points. My clinical interest in Jen and other women whose cases I will cite has to do with what initiates recovery and how people have been able to use that initiation in becoming themselves It is a view that unites illness, relatedness and therapeutic insight in a changed image of what it means to be a woman. So my interest is as much in the unpredictable, the surprising, the mysterious and the metaphorical

as it is in the symptomatic This interest did not begin with
Jen but it was confronted by Jen.

Over the weeks Jen and I struggled together with the
compulsive, tenacious grip of her infantile tendencies She
was not simply immature, she was also grossly unaware
of the implications of her lack of personhood excepting
when it 'hurt'; that is, when she was sick, attacked,
ignored, kicked out, abused But I was also 'young' in my
profession and found it difficult to maintain a continuity of
approach, to command sufficient resources to deal with
her bewildering fantasies, her dreams, her cunning resistances, her seemingly 'bedevilled' way of acting out unconscious impulses – to find time enough, to find a way to
manage with the constraints of her situation, to locate
sympathetic doctors when needed in emergency, to keep
my own sense of balance and perspective, and at times to
recover that most necessary of therapeutic ingredients,
patience

But we persisted. Resources were obviously limited and
relationships strained, yet, there appeared to be no other
choice excepting to have her committed to what would
have been a long-term stay in something like an asylum.
That I was unwilling to do. So we stuck it out for two and a
half years and the culmination of the first phase of our
work together sparked an awareness now many times
reinforced that even when outer support is lacking, something can arise from the hidden layers of psyche that
initiates a person to a new way of seeing herself and of
being in the world, neither erasing nor correcting her
pathology but incorporating it into a changed person.

The first time I said quietly to Jen, 'You are a woman', I
saw her wince. She immediately shifted position, turned
away, frowned and looked down When I caught her
looking at me again, her eyes were smouldering and she
appeared altogether angry and resentful, as if deprived of
a much needed imaginary object on to which she had
projected her security. Later she could say testily, 'I don't
like it if you use those words; girl, woman, female and all

that.' But I persevered, not in a defensive or argumentative way, but simply acknowledging and reinforcing her awareness that her gender was feminine This could be referred to as the period of 'gender acknowledgment', excepting that Jen herself never volunteered acknowledgment I was the one who saw her as feminine, sometimes daring to address myself to a girl child who had appeared and spoken in her dreams She permitted this; that was all.

Much, much later when Jen was sufficiently aware of differentiation to recognise personifications of part selves, she identified a kind of little demon inside her, an *enfant terrible* of iron will and tenacity who was possessed of irascible thoughts and tempers. He it was, she said, who provoked her to outrage and commanded such obstinate violence as she often displayed. When she described him, he had all the characteristics of a Rumpelstiltskin. I was persuaded, however, that his influence could not be assuaged by comparison or knowledge that was other than self-knowledge; he was a living force. When she constructed a wooden figure of him, out of his head sprouted fifty nails (by then she was in her fiftieth year), positioned and bent to hang over his ears, obstructing his eyes Locked into a perpetual grimace, her inner figure was given the name of Little Nailhead.

'But you are more than just Little Nailhead. He's not all of you,' I maintained. Still, it was many weeks before she could acknowledge any kind of impoverished 'other' enough to admit it might be feminine and eventually speak of it self-consciously as She. Its presence was remote, intangible, almost beyond reach. After a fit of temper when she had bashed up a chair, she could say, 'I was being Little Nailhead', but at no time did she volunteer, 'I am She'.

It was Christmas and we had worked together for nearly three years. My practice would be closed for the holidays. She had seen me for her last appointment before the break. I was with another patient when mid-way through an analytic hour my phone rang. I picked up the receiver and heard Jen's voice. 'Excuse me', she said. 'I know you are probably working but I had to tell you something before I went home' (where she had no access to a phone).

'What do you want to tell me?' I asked.

'I want to tell you that I took her into the city and gave her a Christmas present,' she replied softly

'What did you give her?' I inquired.

There was a pause. 'It took courage and all my money but I put holes in her ears and I bought her gold rings to wear so she'd remember she's a woman for ever and ever', Jen said.

There are several responses which could occur to an analyst, any of which would reflect the person's own orientation But I am not only a woman and analyst; I am also someone with an interest in and a limited experience of anthropology. My response reflected that as well I had been taken unawares and impressed, startled and touched. I fell silent for several moments after the receiver was put down and before resuming conversation with that other person who was in the room, I remember asking myself, 'But how did she know what to do, the rite that *had* to be gone through?'

Nicole was a girl child; there was no doubt about it. She was as lovable as a doll. She was pretty, *beguiling* would be the better word – blush-pink cheeks, dimples, a laughing mouth, blue, blue eyes that sparkled as if with sunlit rain when she wept, long, sweeping hair, yes, 'hair the colour of raven's wings' Hers was a *puella's* charm; she was ever youthful There was an air of innocence about her, an open trust, a sense of unblemished purity She had attracted attention and elicited admiration from the time she had been born. She was adored, applauded for her looks as well as her artistry, and her father's darling.

Nevertheless, speaking in real terms, Nicole could no longer be called a child. She was a woman of thirty-three, a performer of note and married. As a husband she had chosen a male likeness to herself for he was also handsome, a musician, and they often appeared on the same platform. Together, also, they had built and furnished a dream house.

Of late, however, Nicole had begun to find the rigours of international tours excessively demanding and in conflict with her fantasies of settled, harmonious family life. Her interest in her husband had begun to pall, she was attractive and attracted to other men Her presenting symptom was an inability to maintain her performance level She said that she felt a shadow had suddenly fallen over her marriage, her future and her career. 'It's as if the sun has slipped behind a cloud', she said wanly. To recover the sun she sought analysis.

In analysis one expects to work with dreams. Analysis is frequently referred to as 'analysis of the unconscious' and the unconscious is revealed by dreams. Freud spoke of dreams as the *via regia* to the unconscious. Yet Jung wrote, 'The *via regia* to the unconscious is not the dream but the complex, which is the architect of dreams and of symptoms.'[1] So analysis can also be described as the process of 'coming to terms with one's complexes'. It is often triggered by an inner condition, one could say a compelling image, that takes hold of and dominates conscious life

As a consequence, disturbances in human relationships, everyday happenings and decisions consciously lived but without reference to their unconscious implications, events that occur with such startling synchronicity that they convey a feeling of otherworldly and irrational intervention, sudden illnesses or habits compulsively repeated can provide apt and arresting evidence of unconscious processes at work as well as and along with one's dreams. The state of one's business or profession can mirror the state of one's unconscious life. Analytic work attempts to establish a relationship with such symbolic statements whose counterpart is the complex, to complete the one-sided metaphor which neurotic illness mutely expresses. And, when insight is achieved, as in the case of

Jen, it is as if a new point of reference is revealed in the person. What then transpires is more akin to transformation than progression.

The compelling imagery of Nicole's life centred on her father. Psychologically speaking, her childhood relationship with him had neither changed nor been made conscious. Though she could hardly have admitted it, he and not her husband was the great love of her life. And it was not only the personal father who was implicated. She evidenced an unwonted ability to project power, authority and prestige on to other men as well; her elder brothers, for example, lovers, teachers, fellow artists, composers and conductors especially. Live or dead, each was invested with something of the romantic hero and to each she offered herself as real or imagined devotee To a remarkable degree, with her stage presence and as a public figure she fulfilled the role of spiritual consort. She was the performing artist's pin-up girl.

In her own words and not surprisingly, the shadow that had now fallen across Nicole's life was that she 'couldn't lift a finger' to her instrument This was a matter of some anxiety for she was not only gifted and acclaimed but she held very high standards for herself. Her ambitions were lofty; her judgments harsh. She described heights of performance as 'beyond compare'. Certain concerts were 'out of this world'; she anticipated moments of 'inexpressible joy'. In light of such standards, her present condition was untenable. But, nevertheless, there was a schedule to be maintained, contracts to be fulfilled, agents to be satisfied, audiences waiting.

Our work began in the grip of such obvious demands In contrast to the first hours spent with Jen, there was no possibility of turning immediately to the fecund, mysterious regions of the maternal unconscious for nourishment. Instead, we were plunged into the masculine and patriarchal realm of practical decision-making occasioned by the abrasive necessity to maintain an everyday working existence. It was a struggle to find psychological resources for the life of which Nicole was capable, let alone what she envisaged. Moreover, I suspected that behind such an overvalued and glamorised exterior there lurked an unconscious fear of ageing and death. Her shimmering fragility betrayed it

It would have been interesting to see what might have happened if Nicole had undertaken analysis with a man. I sometimes wondered about this but, as it turned out, it's possible that what transpired was facilitated by her having chosen a woman I doubt that the speed with which things changed would have been the same had her analyst been male. Resistances might have been too high or dependencies too difficult to acknowledge; whereas, she felt secure enough to confide in me almost immediately. She disclosed that all was really not well between herself and her husband. Neither was he the prince of her fantasies nor, in short, could she hold him.

Again, it is not my purpose to report the hour-by-hour development of this case in detail. Suffice it to say, we worked with the central complex, keeping in mind but not directing our attention to the presenting symptom itself Nicole was being rejected for the first time by a man, this was where it hurt and this was where her emotional and psychic energy were concentrated.

In classical Jungian terms, Nicole had a functioning ego and a more than adequate performing persona. What she did not have was a sense of her own ability related to her creative potential but realistically commensurate to her talents, what is identified as *animus* strength; and, so, she was unable to affirm a sense of inner worth by sustained outer performance Again, this was a weakness attributable to the nature of her central complex. Without assurance of strong masculine support, competence eluded her. She depended upon teachers, critics, other father figures and lovers. The path to her recovery of individual competence was graphically summarised in the process of divorce: divorce from her husband, yes, but again, psychologically speaking, divorce from all previous lovers as well, those with whom she maintained an ongoing relationship of an unconsciously incestuous and supportive nature.[2]

There are many times when an analyst is required to act in the role of a 'good enough mother'; with Nicole I felt called upon to be a 'good enough father'. We had to recognise that the time had come for her to leave her previous lovers and that she had the strength to do it. In fact, I had to reaffirm that awareness, once it had been acknowledged. Hesitantly and then somewhat more confidently over a period of about ten months, however, she began to take the necessary steps toward acceptance of separation, property settlement, and, finally, divorce itself, counselled and guided by a competent firm of solicitors. The major emotional hurdle in all this was symbolised by her having to move out of her dream house. She made short-term arrangements to live as a guest with friends, had a more sustained period of communal living and then, finally, signed a lease for a flat which could be sublet to other musicians if she chose and when she was away.

Looked at from a behavioural point of view, Nicole made progress and if our goal had been the building of sufficient ego strength for her to establish a life on her own, there was proof that therapy was successful. But had it been? She still went home for the occasional night or dropped in for longer periods if her husband were around. Together the two of them had again planted a lovely garden. Decisions about dividing possessions, furniture and knick-knacks became long drawn-out and tedious Eventually and perhaps not surprisingly, she allowed him to take over her share in the house, albeit with a fair and equitable, though not over generous payment. He loved it, she said, and she couldn't bear to think of his being deprived of it.

Throughout this tense and difficult period, Nicole observed a correct but reserved professional relationship with me, demanding support and counsel but at the same time questioning (though never actually defying) my critical judgment. What she wanted was a new father – or was it her old one? She became more withdrawn as time passed, irritable, somewhat petulant and tearful without obvious reason. She was having afterthoughts and I wondered whether the analytic relationship would hold. Yet, whatever her mood, she came nevertheless, promptly and predictably, regularly on Tuesdays and Fridays.

– Until the Tuesday when she rang and announced, 'I won't be coming today but I'll see you next time.' She gave no reason for cancelling her appointment. I became curious but on Friday she arrived as scheduled Looking somehow carefree and at ease, more so than I had ever seen her, she began to speak almost as soon as she sat down.

'I'm sorry I stood you up last time', she said, 'but I just couldn't make it. My flatmate is on holiday, as you know. I've been on my own for three weeks, I've had a lot of time to think and when I woke up that morning I knew exactly where I was going It wasn't here!' She hesitated and then, 'I went home', she admitted, anxiously awaiting my reaction.

By now it was August. Divorce proceedings had been finalised in late May. She hadn't been back to the house since, so far as I knew, but apparently she had retained a key. Her former husband was away on an extended concert tour.

It had taken three days to complete what she had set out to do. She had cleaned the place from top to bottom. She had mowed the lawn, pruned the hedge and weeded the garden. She had forced herself to do these things, she said. She had cried a lot but she had forced herself to sleep in the house alone each night, as well.

When her task had been completed at last, on the evening of the third day, she had gone out and gathered flowers from the garden, brought them in and arranged them in all her favourite places. The house was beautiful, she said. She had then bathed and dressed and packed her bag. But, before she had left, during the long twilight of the still evening she had drawn her instrument from its case, lifted her fingers and played a recital of favourite pieces. When she closed the door at last, she put her key through the letter-box, leaving the home-no-longer-hers behind, she felt, forever.

The incident had affected the young woman with the power of a strong dream. As she related the story, her words conveyed a natural sense of drama without overtones of her former self-consciousness. From the report I felt that, doing these things, she must have recovered something close to the spontaneous spiritual activity related to poetry and music and called *mythologia* by the early Greeks. There was authenticity and authority in what she conveyed. There wasn't a clinical label to attach to this happening but it was clearly initiatory. She had conducted a funeral rite for the death of a romantic childhood fantasy and, so doing, had reached a new stage of life. 'If a person wants to achieve a real relationship with what *is*, it must first take place,' I remembered.[3]

Such brief notes do not summarise the full course of Nicole's analysis, nor should I suggest that the incidents I report were final But they were decisive and this is what intrigued me. As with Jen, this was a transformative happening which arose spontaneously and, although unplanned, it summarised and articulated what had been disclosed to the subject in the course of her endeavour thus far. The ceremony was not regressive; it did not hark back to previous times or a more primitive state of being. Or, even if it did, like a dream, it was precisely attuned to the present; something, unfortunately, that cannot be said of many rituals in current use today.

In conversation with other analysts I learned that my analysands were not the only ones who enacted such rites; neither, of course, is the practice confined exclusively to women. But I have been particularly interested in the spontaneous ceremonies devised by women because of what they have shown me about the distinctive pattern of feminine transformation as well as for what they have revealed about what appears to be essential for the formation and transformation of psychic imagery This is an ongoing life-long process in all of us and it is appropriately the concern of depth psychologists and analysts along with doctors and priests

As the case of Nicole indicates, action, image and implication are constellated simultaneously when the time is ripe, psychologically. It is too bad, I feel, that earlier generations of Jungians have emphasised initiation as an heroic endeavour and have stressed its primary importance for strengthening the ego itself. This is only part of its impact Initiation pertains to the disclosure of mystery at the same time it informs. In Jungian terms, it deepens an awareness of the self even as ego consciousness is extended.

But the timing of individual needs does not always coincide with the accepted observances of society This was one thing that made Nicole's enactment so impressive. She could not any longer have found in any existing social institution, religious or civil, a containing vessel for her childhood's funeral. To complete it she had had to be alone and to draw upon both female and male components within herself, that is to say, to become a woman, she had had to take authority for so doing. She had done it now in a unique and individual way. She was no longer a girl; she was a woman, herself and alone.

It was my awareness of her aloneness that prompted me to visit Lisa in the clinic only a few hours after the abortion had been performed. Beyond the rush of holiday traffic and out of the hustle of pedestrians I stepped into the semi-darkness and silence of the annex at the rear of the hospital There on the second floor, about a dozen beds were lined up, close enough together for their occupants to share the one available television. I spotted Lisa at the far end of the room; she was the only one who wasn't watching the show She was attempting to read which

made her seem even more remote and separated from her
fellow inmates

As I entered, obviously an outsider, looks of surprise
and suspicion were exchanged up and down the line.
When I approached Lisa's bed, her neighbour shrugged
and turned her face to the wall. Otherwise, eyes remained
fixed upon the screen. No sound, no comment, no word,
nor any suggestion of an emotional response was given. I
had entered a liminal, transitional world. The place had
the anonymity of a waiting-room at an air terminal.

'The girls', as Lisa later referred to them, had all arrived
at about the same time that morning. One after the other
they had received their abortions. They would spend the
night at the clinic and leave together early next day, releas-
ing their beds for an incoming group. I subsequently
learned that none of the women communicated with any
of the others by way of more than pleasantries during her
stay. No one complained; no one betrayed any overt feeling and no-one identified herself by other than her first
name.

'You are like a visitor from another world', Lisa re-
marked. 'I feel a bit like that myself,' she volunteered She
stared at me. She said she had never been so surprised to
see anyone in her life. 'It isn't that it's you. It's that
anyone, *anyone* would bother,' she kept repeating.

I handed her a book that I'd heard her say she wanted to
read sometime. We spoke in hushed tones about ordinary
things for about half an hour and then I left, stepping back
into that other 'just as if nothing had ever happened'
world outside. When we next saw one another, Lisa reported that 'the girls' had asked if I were her mother to
which she had replied, 'Maybe'.

Perhaps I was acting as Lisa's mother at that time,
maybe that was why I had gone to visit her, thereby
breaking a cardinal rule of my own practice but wanting to
maintain a sense of human relatedness at a difficult moment. She was a long way from home; she had conceived
under conditions which were inexplicable to anyone else

or even to herself just then, her family and associates at work thought she was away on holiday. But in truth, she was estranged and cut off, frightened and doing her usual thing of trying to put on a brave face and cope.

My appearance had interrupted Lisa's performance, though fortunately not enough so as to dislodge her mask of composure. I had merely wanted to express, 'This isn't all there is to it, you know. There is another world of people elsewhere, some of whom you may not have noticed but who have noticed you and care.' She got that message and with a part of her being she received it, though only with a part. Nevertheless, that part both received and remembered it. It was reinforced later

Lisa was thirty-six, able, yet unfulfilled. When we first met, it looked as if she might spend her life at home. Possibly she would rise to a top position in her field, which was social welfare; she would then see her parents to their graves, perhaps inherit the house in which she now had her own rooms and then she would settle into retirement. This seemed the most likely thing to happen even though she had potential and gave evidence of more wide-ranging interests.

Twice Lisa had tried to improve her lot by moving to another branch of the helping professions. Before I saw her analytically, she had attended a series of introductory lectures which I had given on Jungian psychology. Apparently what I had said had suggested to her another way and, possibly, a different outcome to her life's story. She wasn't sure she could risk looking closely at herself or trying to analyse what was wrong but she thought she'd give it a try. So, on the last evening of the course, she had snuffed out her cigarette in time to ask for my address and phone number before she caught the bus When she came to my consulting room, she said she had decided to explore further whether analysis could do anything for her.

Lisa was not incapable of feeling, but it was as if she had never discovered her feelings. More than once she reminded me of a picture of The Princess in the Glass Coffin

in my book of Grimm's fairy tales. She could be seen and
could see through to another world, but nothing and no
one could reach or touch her. So, she remained remote
and unawakened.

The story of her early childhood revealed that Lisa was
one of two children; she had a younger brother. Soon after
he was born, the family moved south to the outskirts of
London, a move precipitated by bankruptcy and the
necessity for her father to make a new start in different
surroundings When she was three and her brother not
much more than a year old, both children were put in an
institution for the duration of long drawn out though not
serious illnesses which their mother felt were too much for
her to handle. So, for a year and a half Lisa had hardly
seen her parents and by the time she returned home, she
was almost ready to begin school. School necessitated yet
another move and separation from the family.

While away, feeling bewildered and abandoned, she
learned to conform to what was asked of her by the
institution. She was quiet and well behaved, while at the
same time, she indulged in a private life of vivid fantasy.
From the time she was very young she learned to cope
with her loneliness by dis-associating from what was happening around her. That she found too overwhelming,
emotionally

It is hard to imagine Lisa's shouting, running, shoving,
laughing, pushing, being naughty. She never remembered doing these things as a child. All had been control-
led. Whimsy, affection, curiosity, worship and wonder,
excitement or exuberance were frowned upon both at
home and in her 'homes away from home'. Only life in the
inner world was permitted to be spontaneous and this was
one of the things that later attracted her to Jung. She had
read in his autobiography that he found meaning in intro-
verted play. She wanted to test whether this were true;
and, if it were true, she wanted to lay hold on meaning so
that she could feel that she mattered and begin to live
before it was too late.

With the same attitude she had applied to survival, she later set about providing an adequate education for herself, a career and some sort of social life. She had a good mind and found no difficulty in making her way academically. Competence in caring then became the hallmark of her social welfare work. She learned to administer human problems and fairly soon was advanced to the post of head of department

Socially, she drew her own boundaries, was a good cook, saw her own guests, took evening classes and learned to play the guitar, was convivial but not loud. No one could say that anything about her ever 'hung loose' but she had boy friends Peter, the father of her child, was not her first admirer.

Lisa was a dependable committee member, a good person to fill out a party, a reliable friend, a loyal companion. People used her and she knew it For example, one boy friend had pleaded with her to marry him after they had lived together for two and a half years but she had asked the relevant question, 'Are you thinking of me as your wife or your therapist?' Wherever she was, at home or in the office, people 'came by' but she made sure that they didn't 'get in' until Peter appeared. Peter the Parson, she called him.

In contrast to an outer life which was rather humdrum and ordinary when she began analysis, Lisa's inner life was fascinating. Here one could easily observe a compensatory process at work. Dreams were colourful and insistent. She painted and was surprised at what emerged – in particular, the appearance of a quasi-mythological scene, a ruined temple – of Artemis or Diana? And she had a vision, startling to her, a vision of angelic radiance. 'But I'm not religious!' she insisted. 'How could I be? God doesn't know I exist.'

Such things occurred, yet, for several months, nothing seemed to happen that would establish a conscious relationship between Lisa's night-time imagery and her daytime world My own work with her was directed to the encouragement of feeling and a felt response. There was a danger that she could become a very able textbook interpreter of psychological processes but still remain cut off from human emotion. That seemed not only undesirable but dangerous. What would penetrate her serene, remote reserve, so that she would be released to become a person? Companionship was obviously missing. I, too, welcomed the arrival of Parson Peter

Peter the Parson was fun. He had his emotional and financial difficulties but he also had a sense of humour and added a light touch to Lisa's existence. He took her to jazz concerts, booking them to dovetail with the end of Evensong. He was not a city person, hadn't been born a Londoner, and he enjoyed teaching Lisa provincial songs, stories and sayings. His own parents had been killed when he was very young and he felt he had also missed out on having a childhood So this was his chance, he and Lisa could be children together They began to play and she began to laugh.

It must have been on a weekend break that the child was conceived for both Lisa and Peter were more than usually constrained about maintaining propriety around her colleagues and in his parish. Here, again, she conformed to the protocol that was prescribed and adjusted to what society demanded even in regard to its dictates as to when or how she would be loved. She responded, that is, calmly and predictably, without any outward show of rebellion. She didn't want trouble. She showed a cool exterior and maintained a guarded defence of 'thus far and no further'. She was not naive, however, and it seemed a genuine trick of nature that she became pregnant

Confronted with the news, she didn't appear to be unduly surprised, excited or pleased. It simply did not seem to occur to either herself or Peter that the child could become a living part of their lives. As soon as her pregnancy was confirmed, with Peter's knowledge Lisa made arrangements for abortion and shortly afterward visited the clinic

When she returned to work, Lisa's manner was all the more self-contained, though privately and in the confines of my consulting room, she did grieve. I became her companion in mourning, honouring the tears made no less sufferable by the awareness that they were shed for the lost child that she herself had never been. A life that had been warm and begotten had had to be rejected and refused There had been no other way, as she saw it. But, 'why?' she asked. 'I told you God doesn't know I exist.' She struggled but found no relevant and satisfying answer to her questions.

She had not been a church-goer and, as I have indicated, had quite scrupulously avoided being seen in the parish of Parson Peter. Therefore, I was genuinely surprised one Saturday when I heard her announce, 'You ought to know. I'll be going to church tomorrow. It's All Souls Sunday and Peter wants me there'

After the abortion, apparently Peter had had to face his own suffering but he had also seen and been moved by Lisa's tears. So, at some point, he insisted that they choose a name for the child they had conceived and had chosen to abort. On that All Souls Sunday when he read the names of children who had died during the year, he read the name of Lisa's child along with the others And, later, when the congregation moved out into the churchyard to pray for those who had died unconfirmed, the child was mentioned in the prayers. Here was recognition that it had lived and died. Moreover, Lisa's motherhood and his fatherhood, her child and their loss were thereby acknowledged that day before God.

In Lisa's psychological life the service on All Souls Sunday marked a death, a birth and a *coniunctio* or union of opposites. As man, lover and priest, Parson Peter had unconsciously become the instrument for awakening the slumbering passion of her body and her sleeping soul. He had cracked the glass which had encased her emotions. The service was a symbolic christening of herself along with her child and it symbolised her marriage as well. The

unique ceremony was an authentic image of an inner and
psychological happening and it provided the missing element, the spiritual counterpart of her stay in the clinic

In the case of Lisa it is hard to follow a progression of
analytic work from diagnosis to treatment and this is one
reason why I have chosen to report it. It revealed still
another dimension to my researches, reinforcing for me
Jung's insight that the image alone is the object of the
patient's striving and the analyst's search.[4] Certain archetypal continuities are observable and comparable between
any two analysands, but that is all. The clinical picture can
only be descriptive and generalised for each individual
arrives at his imagery by a different route. A person
approaches insight in his or her own way and realises it in
his or her own terms and time

The nature of the evidence we seek is evidence of encounter with the living archetype, not verification of a
conceptual definition already formulated. Such evidence
is available only symbolically and it is conveyed by way of
images. These images are incomplete without awareness
of their connection with a meaning which includes more
than the person. Yet, the analyst deals with persons for
'the sole and natural carrier of life is the individual'.[5]
Dealing with persons makes powerful and unpredictable
demands upon an analyst's abilities to relate individually,
since we therapists are not just agents of treatment but
fellow participants in a process of psychological change.

Why had Emily come to me? This was a question that I put
to myself after visits which were so time-consuming, re-
quiring such effort and made under such obvious
hardship. She was an elderly woman, hardly at an age
when one would expect her to embark on a long analysis.
During the first hour that we spent together we joked
about work in the fourth quarter of life. What was the
meaning of her undertaking this now? Why was she doing
it?

Yes, what was it all about? Emily had had other

analysts. She had always chosen carefully, working
steadily with men of recognised ability and good repute.
The first and most significant of her therapists had been a
well-known psychiatrist/analyst now long since dead. She
had seen this person regularly for years; but she had also
had more than two decades to work through the mourning and grief engendered by that loss.

Emily, her father's favourite, had been a girl of unusual
promise and had become a woman of great beauty. Married during a period of prolonged national austerity, she
had struggled with the exigencies and hardships of establishing a home, making do, keeping up with social demands and meeting the needs of three small children.
Partly as a consequence of all this, she had suffered an
early breakdown. But, as the children had grown up, way
had opened for her to use her own talents after a fashion
and within the framework of marriage to a somewhat
prestigious, innovative and increasingly successful
businessman.

Her husband was deeply devoted to her and solicitous
of her welfare despite her more artistic temperament and
somewhat different outlook. She was well provided for.
There had been setbacks and difficulties, one child had
died before reaching adolescence and another was chroni-
cally ill. The third, now adult, was divorced from his wife.
Still, so far as I could ascertain, Emily seemed to face
nothing more terrible than confronts most ageing persons.
On the whole, her life appeared to have been relatively
smooth.

No one is ever completely analysed but Emily had been
well analysed and evidenced an ability to recognise and
take into account unconscious promptings. What, then,
had prompted her to come to me, I wondered Had she
had a forewarning of terminal illness or accident, either
her own or that of someone close to her? She was a very
contained person. Was there something withheld? 'What
was it all about?' I asked again; and, importantly and
repeatedly, 'Why me?'

This time Emily said that she had consciously set out to find a woman analyst. More than that she could not articulate, except to express a longing for release and to say that at the approach of death this long-denied wish had become an urgent necessity. She wanted release from something that felt like a band wound tightly around her chest, as she expressed it. 'It's a band I've worn much of my life, upwards of fifty years, I would guess', she said. Twice she had been seriously ill. She could accept death, she thought, but she wasn't ready to die. There was more to be lived, lived psychologically, she insisted. Whatever individuation was, she felt it wasn't completed, certainly not yet for her.

Acknowledging this yearning for release, with foresight Emily had selected me. Yet, while it was I who was destined to accompany her on the ritual path that lay ahead, it was she who led me to a deeper understanding of what it means to be a woman and analyst. Somewhere I might appear to be strong and experienced while she felt herself to be still young and needy; yet I was also youthful and inexperienced in an area where she was wounded and had access to greater wisdom. Our complementarity encouraged a surprising psychological interchange, a full and continuous affirmation of the one in the other. In retrospect, I feel that Emily and I initiated one another.

Our exchanges grew in significance without our fully realising what was happening at first. They took place within analytic hours, sustained and gently guided by dreams which stimulated our conversations and focussed our attention. As analysis got under way, the exchanges evoked a long confession and abreaction on Emily's part, exposing her to all that involves of suffering, shame and guilt as well as release. This was purposeful abreaction which came as a prelude to integration for more complete and meaningful living and loving as well as dying.

As I look back over my case notes, I realise in how many ways Emily's case could be interpreted, in what a multiplicity of ways it might have developed. And I ask,

'Would any of them have been wrong?' My answer is always, 'No, not wrong. The errant ways are several. The only possible mistake is avoidance of the opportunity'. Because of her age, particularly, there was a temptation to look at all that happened as preparatory for death itself without according it the individual meaning and promise which belongs to living one's death rather than dying to life. But whenever I was tempted to do this, some cunning hand seemed to intervene as if with silent intention. We were not allowed to escape.

It took a while, however, as much as a year or more before certain dreams broke upon Emily with demanding implication, redirecting her attention to something other than the daily round so essential and essentially reflective of a life prepared to be lived fully as the one she was and no other. Many things needed doing: relationships and possessions had to be sorted and set aside so that her now limited energies could be applied to different purposes.

Then, at last, she dreamed:

I am out of doors. It is night. I am walking on a hillside. There is a street and I am on it.

I start to sing loudly in rhythm with my walking and I swing a veil in my right hand, swing it around in circles as if I need to do this. I seem to see light at the edges of the material as it circles round and perhaps I feel just a little bit proud and comforted because of my ability to produce these flashes. But, then my heart lurches. Coming toward me is myself, a ghost, wraith-like, white in outline – I, floating and over there.

To my surprise I have an urge to help this ghost instead of avoiding it. I stretch out my hand, saying 'Emily', appealing for it to come toward me even as I move closer to it.

Emily saw me somewhat erratically, depending upon the availability of her energy and transport. This arrangement was part of an acknowledgement that I was a professional companion but she was the one in charge of her life. Despite the frequency or infrequency of her visits, however, several analytic sessions intervened between the report of this dream and her arrival on a hot summer afternoon when I met her, as usual, at the door. 'Oh, I am glad to be here,' she said. 'It was so hot in the underground!' She then asked abruptly, 'But how are you?'

'I am all right', I replied, 'but I have had rather a lot to deal with lately, all things considered, and I'd be less than honest if I didn't also say that I am tired and quite ready for a break We all wilt sometimes.'

The consulting room is small and close on a hot day, but there is no-one else in the flat during working hours and, so, there is complete privacy I can leave the door open. That afternoon, however, Emily closed it firmly behind her. She sat down and immediately began to sob After several minutes she caught her breath for long enough to say, 'I am *glad* you said that. I didn't know whether I'd ever say what I really want to say to anybody, but that lets me say it.'

'I respect you and all your colleagues, including every analyst I've ever known', she went on, when she could. 'I owe my life to you and to them and I know you can't let all of us inside your lives. But sometimes I do feel you (and I am speaking of analysts as a group) could be a little bit more human and admit that you have problems too, that all is not always OK and you aren't always on top of it – that, as you've said, you wilt sometimes You're the first one I've ever heard admit it.' She continued to weep. 'It's hard being an analysand, you know, and having no chance for human contact with someone you love and are supposed to trust.'

'Yes, I know it's hard', I replied. She looked very frail. I took her hand. She looked up and nodded, her wet eyes searching my face for permission. Hand-in-hand, we progressed toward a long denied destination.

'The tears come from a wound that goes back forty years', she said, and proceeded to report the first of her analytic loves. She withheld nothing. The radiance of her old age suggested her ripeness in young womanhood If her excitement and vulnerability made her sparkle now, she must have been quite irresistible then. Her disclosure revealed the question faced by every woman (and not only in analysis), faced usually more than once in a lifetime, a question the answer to which is decisive for her relationship with men from then onward. 'Why couldn't he face it?' was all she asked

'He'd made his decision; but what was needed was for him to acknowledge it. He didn't have to choose *me*, but why couldn't he say he had chosen someone else? Why was I abandoned?' She was perplexed and looked at me searchingly. I had no answer.

She knew that she had been attractive; many men had told her so. And, with a wisdom that had instinctively informed her woman's being, she had known he had been attracted to *her*, or unconsciously seduced, which she could admit He was seeing her several times a week. He gave evidences of special attentions, allowing for extra-professional favours. She grappled and assumed that he also grappled, with the tensions that had been aroused, both inner and outer, the conflicts between the so-called 'real' world of a marriage to a man she could not think of leaving and that other so powerful pull toward someone who appeared to be 'so much more' She felt the magnetism of a love that her partner seemed to acknowledge, tacitly, and acted upon. She followed his lead. He was the doctor; she was only his patient.

On another summer's morning long ago, repressed passion had been at its height. She relied upon him; he gave her no reprieve She was locked out and locked in, as she said. Feeling wretched and unmet, she had left finally and on the way home, to divert herself she had picked up a newspaper. There she had read of his engagement to his secretary. But in the weeks that followed, until she herself brought up the subject, it was never mentioned.

She lashed out in anger 'Why, for heaven's sake, can't analysts acknowledge they are humans? If they could, we would be able to love them and appreciate them even

more And maybe we'd have courage to believe that being
human could also somehow mean being more like them.
But they cut themselves off and we're left alone where it
hurts the most and where we're least capable of fending
for ourselves.'

I was Emily's first woman analyst and, therefore, in
some way and to some extent, relieved of male responsibility. I had also admitted to being human that day. I also,
admittedly, had heard what she said, without blame to
anyone but also without refutation or denial So I was face
to face not only with her anger but also with the evidence
of a life curiously impoverished by lack of trust in man as
well as analyst and, consequently, with a life somewhere
withheld as woman. That she could say it at last, confronting me on equal terms, might release her. But one doesn't
marry with the intellectual side of one's nature alone, I
reminded myself. Love in its fullness is also physical. She
had cracked the shell of the professional persona, his and
also mine

When she left, we stood face to face at the door. Spontaneously, we put our hands on each other's shoulders,
our heads inclined toward one another. Our cheeks rested
together. There was silence. We pondered One said,
'Thank you for all you've given me today.' The other
replied 'Thank you for all you've given *me*.' We embraced.

To one of her next sessions she brought a dream in
which she moved forward to face that long postponed and
dreaded confrontation with her former lover. In the dream
I stop her momentarily, asking 'You're not taking the
letter with you, are you?'
The dream reports:

I notice I am in fact holding a folded letter in my left
hand Is it for him, for someone of whom I was very
fond? It is a simple, folded sheet of grey, without an
envelope I must have written it. I look at it and then I
realise that this is a flesh and blood situation – *the written
word on paper just will not do.*

The iron band had snapped; the traumatic wound had

been disclosed. She acted with new authority. Perhaps, of course, what she reported of her former love was a delusion but it was nonetheless real to her and subsequently she had lived in terms of it for many years as wife and mother of a daughter and two sons. In the interval between her silence and speaking she had also transferred to me the impenetrable question, 'Why, for heaven's sake, can't you (he) acknowledge it?' With her words she had inducted me to the necessity for discovering my own standpoint. In every new case involving the maturation of a woman I am reminded of her. Whatever the evidence that is brought, and I am assured it will always be different with every analysand, I hear her speak.

My relationship with Emily, who was living so fully as she prepared to die, opened to me the understanding that the phenomenon of transference cannot be seen in its fullness either as a professional or a purely personal relationship. We depotentiate it if our only interpretation is from a conceptual or methodological, that is to say an intellectual, point of view; but, also, we lose perspective by viewing it solely in personal terms. It is above all a loving human relationship. Only through mutual love are the former constraints of the ego overcome and the authentic personality released. In the union of two creatures of the same nature and of equal significance, yet in every respect distinct, is the creation of the new person, the more complete person, possible.

She could be said to have died young. In after years, she was able to face death more confidently and with greater trust. As for myself, Emily did not teach me about the transference but she did teach me by way of the transference that the disillusioned body withholds its womanly warmth until such time as it can be re-initiated. And there was new comprehension in my subsequent reading of Jung:

> The touchstone of every analysis that has not stopped short at partial success, or come to a standstill with no success at all, is always this person-to-person

relationship, a psychological situation where the patient confronts the doctor upon equal terms, and with the same ruthless criticism that he must inevitably learn from the doctor in the course of his treatment [6]

Amanda did not consciously choose to terminate her pregnany. When at last it was discovered what was wrong, the dead foetus of a five and a half month old child had to be removed from her womb She has spent many hours searching for the grave of the baby. In her fantasy this was a girl and she has given it a girl's name, A .   The death of the child-in-embryo summarised and brought to an end the first half of Amanda's life. She was unprepared for its living, but the dying of her little girl has enabled her to live differently.

Amanda's analysis can be seen as a ritual progression towards integration of that shocking event. Not all of her analytical experience has been with me, however. Previously she worked with a man for an extended period and this prepared her for the advent of meaning in her loss With him her anger was initially vented and a preliminary battle with the one she perceived as a malevolent and angry god was waged By the time she came to me she had effectively won back a rudimentary sense of dignity as a human person with a woman's body.

Amanda means 'fit to be loved', but as a small child, in a home privileged in every other sense, she was deprived of that very thing she most longed for, love. She knew that she longed for it and it hurt not to have it. She was a lonely, restive little girl. What she could offer· beauty, sensitivity, playfulness, intelligence, artistry and an intense, spontaneous yearning to give and receive affection never seemed to gratify her parents. At least, they did not return her affection in the same measure, so she was never affirmed naturally as the one she was. Whatever it is that presides over the destinies of individuals seemed to adjudge that she must claim her name by winning her right to love. It was as if it had been decreed

'I don't know why you were born to me,' Amanda

remembers her mother saying as she dressed her tiny daughter 'You would have done much better as my sister's child!' As it so happened, Aunt Marina, the sister of Amanda's mother, had no little girl, only two lively boys, so Amanda might have taken advantage of the empty place in that family. But she didn't dare; the costs were too high, even when calculated by a nine year old child.

Mother would be jealous, her tongue even sharper, Amanda figured. Better to ask Aunt Marina only for the things she *couldn't* get at home; like lessons in embroidery, maybe a chance to weave on the big loom. Aunt Marina liked to cook. When would she, Amanda, be old enough to make the bread with her aunt? Next summer? Summers she always went to visit her. Making bread would keep her out of the way of those pesky boys. But better not ask; that was too risky. – So a little girl's fantasy ran. Mother would call it teasing and that would make her flare up, as she had a way of doing frequently now that Amanda's brother had been born. That was just the end of Amanda's hopes as a little girl, she said. She had been eight, just starting to have ballet lessons, and that was special. But then he had appeared, robbing her of what time and affection she had felt able to retrieve from her mother.

Seemingly, the birth of her brother had robbed her of a father as well, for, as an infant, the brother had a marked fear of his father and every effort was made to reassure the child that he was accepted – perhaps, even preferred. At least, that is how Amanda saw it and only once, during her adolescent years, did her father give her special undivided attention for any length of time. When she was seventeen, he took her to Europe to visit his former home and relatives and to show her off.

The summer spent abroad and in the company of her father was determinative in Amanda's choice of career. The culture to which she was introduced became the culture of her choice. She could speak her father's native language fluently, perhaps even better than he. She was

already enrolled at university but within a year she transferred to a woman's college within the same system, and
selected as her major subject a field which was related to
her father's country and would necessitate frequent visits
there on her own. She would get a PhD and excel. These
accomplishments both parents would surely applaud, she
fantasised

In their eyes, Amanda did begin to show signs of promise at last. She was not going to settle down in the predictable and conventional ways that they had hoped As a
matter of fact, she had already rejected the boy whom they
had chosen and to whom she had consented to become
engaged But who could tell? Maybe one day she would
become a famous scholar instead. Meanwhile, Aunt Marina was painfully dying of cancer and a life-long pattern of
migraine set in for Amanda herself.

Twenty years later, when I first met this woman, she
had once been married but was now divorced. With her
young husband she had conceived a child but he had
rejected outright the idea of its being born and so that first
pregnancy had been terminated. Despite his personal
frustrations and consequent emotional battering of Amanda, when she finally left this husband, he had followed
her to the place where she had taken up a teaching post on
another continent One of a series of difficult lovers, he
threatened and harassed her for several months, resisting
separation until, clearly, there was no alternative. With
insight she perceived that he struggled with her as if she
were part of himself but he was yet another who couldn't
or wouldn't love Amanda as she was, herself. She found
this awareness hard to tolerate.

Would anyone ever, she wondered, recognise and
accept her as herself and as she was? Following the
divorce, she was pursued by a succession of men, all
of whom were professional colleagues, each of whom
projected on to her the image of his ideal academic partner. Wedded to *academia* rather than seeking a relationship with a human partner, they all preferred to have a

companion similarly committed to an already charted and competitive intellectual journey.

She felt her body was used, her person invaded. Often accused of coldness and infidelity, she would subsequently discover that while she remained faithful, her lovers were having outside affairs. Twice, on the verge of theoretical breakthrough in her own field, she was diverted, her progress interfered with and her research pirated by one or another of these men. She considered herself to have been blackmailed, spiritually and emotionally raped. She was enraged. The scenario of her childhood was repeated.

'Fit to be loved' but who would love her? 'What's wrong with me? Am I a monster or something?' These were questions she brought to analysis. Her startling beauty, her tenderness and natural grace were by now obscured by a mask of resentment and defiance. She needed a mask to defend herself until more adequate inner resources were discovered and developed; or, at least, until Lucian found her. Who or which came first and was the more effective, Lucian or analysis, it is hard to say. They belonged to Amanda and together.

Lucian was a man already fully established in a parallel field of study. He had also been married and divorced. He was now searching for someone with the sensitivity his former wife lacked. Desirous of a warm, responsive partner, captured by Amanda's looks and her personality, affably and persuasively he set out to convince her that she was attractive, attractive to him and, indeed, that he loved her not for *what* she was but *as* she was.

Before they married, it was Lucian who fathered A . . ., the lost but wanted baby. With his encouragement, when Amanda came to see me she was in the final stages of publishing her brilliant, well researched and about-to-be widely acclaimed thesis which had been so long delayed. Lucian was her husband; she was nearing forty, and she wanted to bear him a living child.

Despite her trials, despite her fortitude, despite prior analytic help and despite even Lucian's devotion, Aman-

da still did not seem to have yet been initiated into adulthood however, not as herself, not as Amanda, the unique
woman she could be. She had won through to maturity by
a show of strength, penetrating intellect, superior performance and endurance. She had established a place for
herself alongside men but it was not until the death of
A . . ., her child, that she was shocked into awareness of
having at the same time abandoned something which she
now felt to have been of great value and belonging to
herself uniquely as woman.

Could she recover and in time? She wasn't particularly
strong and she was frightened. Pregnancy was a risk,
emotionally, physically, and also psychologically. She was
often ill Moreover, in order to give birth to a child, she
would be required to say *yes* to something beyond her
control, surprising, unformed and with a nature unde-
clared If she wanted her child, she would need to love it
for its own sake and put that loving first, even before her
own need to be admired and loved herself. It was a lot to
expect that she could be a satisfactory mother when she
had experienced so little of genuine mothering.

And, should this child be denied her, how could she
withstand what she would inevitably interpret as yet
another attack on her person by a dark and ominous god?
There were reasons for my not giving immediate and
unqualified assent to a request for analysis at this time,
questions that related both to herself and to me. Certain
resistances were deeply ingrained. She had withstood
emotional rejection, ordeal and torment; she was wary.
Would she dare to trust ever? Could I withstand sustained
lack of trust?

She had been recommended to work with me by her
gynaecologist. I stopped; I wondered whether I should
take her on. She had had the experience of a previous
analysis which had engendered hope. An important factor
was the constancy of Lucian's love He was a devoted and
positive figure in her life, offering emotional security and
support, though he himself had less faith in unconscious

forces than she had. But, perhaps, after all, Amanda's strongest resource was the unexplored experience of her most recent suffering from which she had received a certain affirmation combined with wound and humiliation.

There were two additional aspects of Amanda's background which impressed me as having psychological relevance as well. The first was the fact that when he had been informed of A . . .'s death, Amanda's father had wept, wept naturally, spontaneously and without restraint, for a long time out of sympathy for his daughter. The second was that she often dreamed of Aunt Marina. In the first, I found moving evidence of a primary feeling bond with father, a male authority figure who had repressed his love but, nevertheless, had found her lovable. In the other was an image of woman that continued to validate and extend her own.

Consideration of these things informed my reflections. No case can be fully explored objectively for no two people ever perceive things in the same way. Who knows how Amanda's mother would have described her little daughter's upbringing? How would Aunt Marina have spoken of her niece, Amanda? What would her father have said, her brother, the head of her department or any of her lovers? In the end, the analyst must work with what she herself perceives, intuits and feels. How far could I myself place my trust in a dark image ravaged by the events of this woman's life? Was it Amanda or I who might not dare to risk belief? These were questions to be acknowledged before I said *yes*.

CHAPTER 2

THEIRS BY RITE

The image alone is the immediate object of knowledge.
Jung, 'Medicine and Psychotherapy'

Jen enacted a ceremony as old as our records of woman. On the eve of her adulthood she secluded herself. When she was ready to emerge and be seen as the one she had become, she accepted symbolic wounding, received the mark of her status, and celebrated. 'With gold rings she was bedecked.' The rite was designed to impress, she would remember it 'forever and ever'.

With reference to theory, I could explain this happening, and as a therapist I could rejoice. I have stated earlier that Jen had been diagnosed as an hysteric and she had an hysteric's propensities for converting psychological necessities into somatic manifestations. But she also had the hysteric's flare for the dramatic; and sometimes she overplayed her part, calling attention to herself by so doing. Psychologically, she had remained in a prolonged, arrested childhood state and so had taken recourse to a wide range of infantile defences; aggression, exaggeration, stubbornness, clowning, vulnerability, naughtiness, helplessness – amounting in the end to an inflation of omnipotence.

In classical Jungian terms, hers was a disturbance of the animus in which the ego was identified with the persona of the 'young boy' Archetypally, she was victim of a mother complex. Hers was a narcissistic character disorder. These were all factors of which I was conscious. They formed the clinical infrastructure of the analysis; and, yet, clinical explications of what had now taken place left me curiously ill at ease.

Traditionally, clinical interpretations made by depth psychologists follow the route taken by an individual in relation to an archetypal disturbance. Clinical investigations are scientific in the sense that their conclusions are based upon hypothesis, observation and testing. The opposite approach is not symbolic but metaphorical, which appears to be psyche's own way of communicating with and reforming itself Symbolism is common to both approaches and analysis partakes of both

Considering these two approaches, clinical and metaphorical, it was from the latter perspective that I now began to approach Jen's case. With a single spontaneous gesture she appeared to have acknowledged an alteration in her life, if not her being And, depending upon her ability to sustain such a spurt of psychological growth, if given a clinical or medical rating, she would certainly achieve a high score. From near to the bottom of her class and off to a poor start, so to speak, she had somehow managed to pass. This itself was no mean accomplishment and in her mother's words, it would certainly be classed as 'good behaviour'. As a narcissistically wounded person, she had at last given evidence of self-worth and valuation She was certainly 'improved' and, again, depending upon the stability of her future progress one day she might conceivably be called 'cured'. But, were that to happen, who other than a doctor would use such a term and what did it convey, I asked myself? Or, supposing she regressed, who or what would be to blame?

Was there a place for rating and judgment here at all, I

wondered. I knew some of my colleagues would say that ultimately Jen would be judged by her own unconscious, objective psyche; others that her life would be measured by the adequacy of her later ego performance or her ability to sustain consciousness of her new-found femininity. These were serious, considered statements but they gave less than adequate recognition to what was involved in Jen's attempt to establish and record truth for and as herself. They said nothing, for example, about the impulse that had prompted the improvisation of this particular act. So I found myself returning to the metaphorical element that had been employed. When confronted with her dilemma and potential, she had not set out to accomplish an heroic feat; neither had she tried to rid herself of an unwanted illness. She had simply enacted an unplanned, image-laden rite.

Certainly I was aware that I had made mistakes in handling the case of Jen, if I looked at it from a clinical point of view. Yet, what had now taken place fulfilled no pattern of clinical predictability; it conformed to no hypothesis of what we could expect if certain things were provided, administered, adhered to. It was an unexpected phenomenon; rating and judgment, whether clinical, theoretical or moral, seemed to accord no place to the fullness of its implications, nor allow for the surprise and joy of the shared human encounter. Apparently doing it and telling me about it had belonged together. Yet the gift hadn't been intended for me The gold rings were for 'her'.

At that time, my awareness of the fullness of what had happened was incomplete. I seemed to have knowledge but somewhere I lacked understanding. Therefore, I could neither adequately comprehend nor yet explain the just-so quality of this incident and the sense of its being so rightly fitting For, symbolically, it was unerringly precise I cautioned myself against trying to make interpretations or presuming to see a meaning beyond the event itself at the moment, however. If it had meaning, that was Jen's to discover and articulate; of that much I was sure.

I suspected that what she had done did not conform to a

model, medical or otherwise, but, rather, was in response
to a fundamental, deep-rooted, perhaps instinctive urge
that had very little to do with her upbringing excepting
insofar as that had provided the setting and the costume
for her act, so as to speak. Whatever had motivated this
performance was an urge sufficiently strong to throw her
back into her prehistory, activating the latent collective
and unconscious memories of what to do and how to do it,
regardless of limitations imposed by outer circumstances.
Yet, it was of concern to me that I could not yet grasp the
full import of what she'd done. If that continued to elude
me, how could I help Jen or anyone else in a similar
position to go further, I wondered, – further, that is, than
to be labelled as ill or 'cured' whether that was a judgment
based upon a medical diagnosis or an hypothesis pertaining to any other theory of collective human behaviour?

The designing urge of this ceremony was individual and
had somehow propelled Jen toward becoming a woman,
herself But, as a woman, she lived on the threshold of
times fraught with societal change and, though neither of
us could have guessed it, she was about to become first a
craftswoman and then an artist whose work would be
noticed and exhibited precisely because she *was* a woman
and was acknowledged to represent woman, not because
she was a 'late developer', deviant or case. What is the
nature of an impulse that can effect something so momen-
tary and yet long-lived; specific and yet wide-ranging; so
personal, as also universal; timely and yet timeless, while
imminent and at once transcendent in the sense that it
transcended her previous condition?

The pursuit of answers to such questions led me ultimately to investigate two parallel imageries; one being the
image of process – how psychological images form, are
incorporated and change; and the other being the image a
woman has of herself Jen's action not only posed unsettling problems but, had I guessed it at the time, illustrated
some of the solutions. And it was in conjunction with these
same problems that the presence of Nicole, whose appearance coincided with that of Jen, was of immediate signifi-

cance. The funeral for her doll's house suggested to me two lines of enquiry, each complementing and completing the other.

The one had to do, as I have said, with process, *how* one becomes a woman The other was concerned with what it *is* to be a woman, psychologically. Both involve imagery and I had to work toward a comprehension of each at one and the same time, for it was in the investigation of the one that I found the key to an understanding of the other. I wonder whether this may not be a psychological truth, namely, that process cannot properly be seen apart from purpose.

From this much of an understanding (that images of process and person are inseparable) it follows that any approach to psyche involves both. Therapy that depends upon application of a technique avoids consciousness of this primary interdependency and immediately becomes either a summary judgment or an attempt at verification of an external hypothesis. In the analytic encounter it is the task of the analyst to be mindful of process; the analysand will remain mindful of person. If, however, one's view of process degenerates into mere fulfilment of a pre-arranged plan or is too closely linked with the goal of personal development, there is avoidance of an encounter with genuine and lasting possibilities of change, change which affects the entire person, soul and spirit as well as body and mind, the kind of change which is more appropriately spoken of as healing rather than cure. In the course of an analysis, images of process and person which coalesce and co-inhabit naturally are made conscious. Therapy attends both to the making of images and our being made by them

By person, however, I do not mean to imply something limited to what is purely 'personal' or revealed by a case record. Rather, it is an image of one's own self that is both more comprehensive and inclusive of what it is like to be human and of this species, female or male psychological-ly. It is an image of one's self in relation and obedience to what one is, intelligible and corporeal. Within that image, one's personal context has a unique function and it is possible to discern individuality.

Here there is need to introduce a further consideration relevant both to the analytic process and to that of maturation consciously pursued or otherwise. It is the concept of 'likeness' to image 'Likeness is consciousness of image and its embodiment *Image* is archetypal and by way of its archetypal promptings excites and invites, in fact, insists upon a personal manifestation of itself. This implies relationship and *likeness* results from a personal response to that or those promptings It is not a question of imitation; a person becomes in part and to the measure that he is able 'like to' the image that prompts and he perceives.[1]

It was for a shift from image to likeness that Jen's ceremony was designed and hence, I understood, it was a rite of initiation. But, though essential to the end, the rite did not achieve the effect (for there was a lasting and effective change in her person); rather, it appears that the image, being archetypal, was itself capable of bringing about the effect that it pre-figured, in whatever form she may have expressed it. But, until the time of her initiation, she remained unconscious of what she was about to realise. She remained unconscious of her personal likeness to woman.

Ceremonies of initiation provide natural metaphors for the process of psychic transformation and, consequently, generations of Jungian analysts have made comparisons between analytic and initiatory practices. Still, by and large, these practices have thus far been explained by reference to a male model, and consciousness, not embodiment, has been emphasised as the goal. This and an over-reliance upon ready symbolic interpretations may at times have served as a rational barrier against confrontation with the range of psychological resources and energy for transformation to which Jen and these other women inadvertently exposed themselves and me with the result that we were forced to wonder and take a close, deep look at what was happening.

The ceremonies employed by all five had certain features that I believe 'caused', in the sense of 'generated', their effectiveness. Moreover, they were 'specific', in the sense of 'designed' to achieve psychological transformation of image along with that of person. That is to say, a changed image and likeness of woman resulted in each instance and these changes apparently occurred coincidentally with the performance of the ceremonies rather than as a result of subsequent interpretation and experience.

Here we have an illustration of the meaning of archetype as it was originally defined, 'a masterstroke that leaves an impress', and we are reminded of the Scholastic's notion that the archetype is a natural image engraved on the human mind, helping it to form its judgments. With curiously psychological overtones, a modern social scientist writes:

The arcane knowledge or *'gnosis'* obtained during the liminal period (of initiation) is felt to change the inmost nature of the neophyte, impressing him as a seal impresses wax, with the characteristics of his new state. It is not a mere acquisition of knowledge but a change of being.[2]

For this to happen, a ceremony must fulfil the needs of the unconscious as well as the conscious self and, so, it becomes ritual. '. if you go into the history of the rite, if you try to understand the whole structure of that rite, including all the other rites round it, then you see it is a mystery that reaches down into the history of the human mind, it goes back very far – far beyond the beginnings of Christianity,' Jung writes [3] For something to have lasted so long it must have served a need in the human psyche. When he wrote those words, Jung was primarily interested in the archaic remnants of such rites, but my interest focussed upon the natural function of rite itself.

In ritual performance, one is released from conventional modes of behaviour or the necessity to conform to a conscious cultural canon; one gives expression to unconscious promptings which require symbolic enactment for disclosure of as yet undisclosed truths. By way of analytic discourse, we search for psychic equivalencies while ritual provides them. It is one thing to consider interpretations of what certain utterances and gestures mean but quite another to be prompted to use them Along with its related disciplines, analytical psychology attempts to summarise in words the ontological mystery that these women could not avoid expressing.

By and large, their particular rituals were personally designed and suited to their unconscious needs; there were few reflections of collective or dogmatic practices. The ceremonies were impromptu, spewing forth as if in answer to a summons from a strong inner force felt to be 'more than human' They came, if you like, as eruptions from that reservoir of archaic memories, symbols and rites which Jung held to be the psychological heritage of all of us, uniting us with our psychic brothers and sisters around the world and throughout all ages, the collective unconscious. But, for Jen, Nicole or Lisa (with the help of Parson Peter), these forms broke into being as if *de novo* and in response to their own individual needs. When the moment came, they had an instinctive 'feel' for what was required As Nicole reported, she knew exactly where she was going and what she was going to do. In this sense, initiation offers very little choice; rather, it announces itself when its time has arrived.

In a scientific age, it is a temptation to look upon the archaic power of such actions as either rudimentary or regressive. As an analyst, my approach to them was as if to living dreams, i e. metaphorical enactments triggered by unconscious impulses and masterminded by as yet unconscious forces The rites were, in each instance, new and creative configurations of the utmost significance for further development in the individual. We took them seriously, respecting both the form (the ritual itself) and its motive force as expressive of the psychological condition and necessity of the person at the moment.

During this stage or phase of analysis, each individual's need for a symbolic as well as a conscious life became more apparent for, symbolically, in these rites each of the women was able to face and express the mystery of which she was deprived in daily life. And, it was upon these occasions, reverted to only as a last resort, that some sort of meaning was implied in the suffering of their day-to-day existences. 'Rituals reveal values at their deepest level . . . men (and women) express in ritual what moves them most.'[4]

Perhaps all experience of ritual is initiatory to a greater or lesser degree but rites of initiation are remarkable for recognition and incorporation of a new relationship between spirit and body as well as society and person. Within their circumscribed space the initiand safely undergoes the often terrifying transformation from image to likeness. This shift takes place whether the ritual is a repeat performance of something that already exists and has been re-enacted for generations or the creation and enactment of a rite that is improvised. But also, 'the more psychological a condition is, the greater its complexity and the more it relates to the *whole* of life, not just as theory but as actual fact, to physiology as well as to the opposites of instinct and a philosophy of life.'[5] Ritual is the natural, necessary and transitional carrier of psychological process.

To use Jung's pragmatic phrase, 'It works.' It works therapeutically in the best sense since it relieves, releases and carries psychic tension during the period of transformation when the image of the formed confronts that of the unformed and the individual is impelled to move toward the yet-to-be-formed. Concerning initiation specifically, however, Jung writes that it occurs when one dares to act against the retrograde law of nature and allows oneself to be propelled toward consciousness. Here he implies that the natural law is synonymous with unconsciousness. Yet, what these women seemed to be responding to was an imperative call for change which arose from *within* their own natures and the call was of sufficient depth, breadth and impact to command both attention and ritualised action.

In this connection, I question the term 'failed initiation', which again implies that at such a time the ego can make a clearcut and final choice as to whether or how to proceed in such circumstances. If the initiatory urge is a natural one and the individual response is to an archetypal impulse, the initiand feels a powerful, nonpersonal pull toward enactment but, at the same time, there are innumerable ways of imagining a response. One does not 'fail' to respond, even when he resists or even withdraws.

To speak of failure is again to make a statement related to collective or conscious goals and it once more implies a standard and a judgment. Rites themselves can only be judged as they are adequate or not for reflection of universal images. Based on the adequacy of the reflection, there are infinite possibilities of individual and psychological choice. But such choices will not necessarily be either conscious or in accord with an accepted or acceptable canon of public behaviour and each will carry in outline, as it were, the form of a yet more adequate likeness to the image which will require initiation at another stage.

None of the encounters, excepting for that of Emily, was marked by much use of clinical or interpretative language Instead, the ceremonies were simply respected as re-articulations of time-honoured ancient rites, necessary and profound. 'These mysteries have always been the expression of a fundamental psychological condition', Jung writes. 'Man expresses his most fundamental and most important psychological condition in ritual . . That explains why we should not change anything in ritual . . . (we) must not allow (our) reason to play with it.'[6] It was an attribute of each of the self-devised ceremonies that it accorded a place to mystery which was both a recognition of a motivating force that was stronger than ego (the master of the masterstroke) and an awareness of there being something more to complete. That is to say, we saw the rite as neither beginning nor end but as an essential part of process.

Immediately, it was more apparent to me as the analyst and observer than it was to the analysand as participant that her rite occasioned an altered attitude to body, time and change. For her, each of the enactments brought with it an initial sense of completion, almost of finality The most frequently repeated phrase was, 'I'll just never be the same again.' Yet, this sense of finality was accompanied by an unsettling premonition that sometime she might well find herself in the grip of a similar summons, though it would be directed to a different end.

As time went on and as had been apparent to Emily and Amanda from the beginning, we saw that even when in the throes of ritual excitement, each of the women had exercised a certain degree of selectivity. Whether knowingly or unconsciously directed to do so, they had 'selected from the mysteries' and allowed themselves to be impressed by only as much as they were able to assimilate psychologically On the one hand, this selectivity could be interpreted as a kind of censorship or conscious choice-making But it bore an individual stamp and could later be recognised as contributing to the emergence of unique personhood, so it was more than an affirmation of the ego In this regard I wonder if too great an insistence upon consciousness on my part could have rendered the rites counter-productive, linking them once again to precepts of accomplishment, failure and guilt.

Thus far I have spoken of ritual almost entirely in logical, conceptual terms, though I have emphasised that it springs from a deep psychological necessity. This could equally well be called a religious necessity for ritual is a confrontation between an 'I am' and a frightening 'I am not'. Therefore, it involves risk and is sobering, often upsetting. Living ritual cannot be compounded as a prescription is compounded of tested ingredients since it provides a place for the individual actively to imagine the unlikely with the aim of *gnosis* or knowledge of the god, the 'I am not', directly perceived as experience. Ceremonies become ritualistic when equal place is accorded to the needs of man or woman and gods or goddesses alike.

Elsewhere I have written that a ritual is a ceremony enacted with a sacred purpose or intent, whether or not one is aware of that purpose or intent Here one is always subject to an overwhelming numinous power capable of destroying or re-creating the individual. To label such a power as 'archetypal' simply draws attention to its forceful and recurrent, imagistic nature. To speak of it as 'entirely other' denies its capacity for embodiment or incarnation. To call it 'God' identifies it with a personal or collective image of the divine already realised in some measure. But, until a person can make that image his own, this is at best only an impersonal and traditional likeness It can be called divine, however, because the power met with is stronger, compelling, numinous and other-than-human although it seems to seek relationship with that which is human.

And it is for the encounter with divine powers that rituals are designed, taking place in a church, a temple or wherever. Such psychological changes as I have described or have been described to me have a religious content, even if the person does not consider himself or herself to be religious and is not a member of a practising religious group. They do not merely help or teach or heal. Fundamentally, they enable a relationship to be established between two different kinds of being, one human, the other divine.

When they were most ordinarily involved as human beings, the five women I have described were also, it seems, most open to spiritual encounter. They had not sought it, did not prepare for or expect it but it emerged as a surprising adjunct to their human and personal dilemma. Afterward, there was acknowledgment of having had a profound experience of mystery and an encounter with meaning that informed their lives. This realisation rather than any kind of religious label that could be attached to it was important to them. We did not often speak of myth in this connection, but it was as if they might already have possessed a pre-conscious awareness of an unfolding of events to which their experience later gave particular credibility, as if to validation of a myth.

Just as the symbol is a falling together of two meanings, the image is a constellation of all meanings essential to the revelation of an archetypal pattern. Ritual, like myth, is symbolically rich because it portrays a cluster of possibili-

ties with many meanings. Only gradually do these meanings become differentiated so that we are able to become
aware of them. Its psychological significance is raised to
consciousness not during the event but afterward. The
initiations that have been reported here were ripe with
meanings which were different for each of the individuals
involved Still, basically, by way of their rites, my analysands discovered something of what it is to be a woman
and themselves, though they did not discover *all* that it is
to be a woman or one's self

With this perception – that meaning unfolds as image
becomes likeness – I found an answer to some of my
questions and reason for my distrust of the psychological
applicability of a purely clinical perspective within which
the meaning is verification of a pre-defined image. Even
the aim of 'consciousness' or 'the realisation of meaning'
can be limiting because it springs from an authority which
is not vested within the person's own psyche. 'Such images as these and statements of meaning are not under
our control', Corbin writes. 'They are, instead psychic
events revealing themselves to our inner experience and
interpreting the reality of a transcendent object.'[7] Imperative and seminal rituals put us in touch with an eternal
myth This is one of their natural functions. They not only
expose subject to object; they also interpret object to subject symbolically.

What occurs when the transcendent interprets itself to
the personal can be viewed either as a personal discovery
of meaning, which is a psychological perspective, or
meaning's discovery of person which is a theological one.
Psychological consciousness, i e. analysis, inevitably links
the two To attempt to live in terms of meaning alone is to
attempt to live only spiritually To live only as person
reduces existence to instinctive materialism.

Initiation rituals give presence and historicity to meaning, though they do not necessarily sanction it. Validation
or confirmation is left to the individual Corbin has also written that to allow for the performance of a rite is to allow

oneself to be placed back in the original situation; to lose
what is present, only to discover it in potential . . . to recall
a past and usher eternity into time.[8] For something cannot
become apparent and remain hidden. When there is greater
knowledge (gnosis) of image, likeness inevitably changes.

In this connection, it is important to note that all five
women were involved with body as well as spirit and it
was demanded of ritual that it contain both. In the case of
Lisa, for example, ritual which pertained to the one was
not completed without the other. It is over-simplifcation to
say merely that the ritual demand 'began' in body or
'showed' in body; or to insist that the rites 'arose' from
body and 'returned' to body. That in some cases they
appeared to do so is a result only of our logical thinking.
But, when meaning was experienced, it was experienced
in and as body, the women reported, and what each
woman knew she knew with her body as well as her
mind, spirit and affection They dealt with religious events
as physical events, not as symbolic of or opposed to matter, and both were recorded as psychic events. Though
forces somatic and spiritual could be seen as autonomous
and primordial powers, they were one in the individual.

Here I am reminded again of Jung's statement on ritual
It is 'a collective or individual attempt to conjure up or
re-awaken those deeper layers of the psyche which the
light of reason and the power of the will can never reach
and to bring them back to life.'[9] This assures that the
moment when one is initiated is a moment of profound
recall, a recalling to oneself of *what* one is as well as *who*
one is. Recurring at somewhat predictable intervals, the
necessity for ritual initiation serves to remind woman
naturally of 'as it was in the beginning' life-long If such
rites are denied, an opportunity for experience of psychic
integration as well as relevance is missed.

There remains to be commented upon only one additional feature that was common to the five ritual enactments when viewed analytically This was the role played
by relationship. When face-to-face with 'the other that she

was not', its power suggested the authority of an image separate and opposed to the woman herself. From the way it was reported, 'the other that she was not' was experienced both as *an* other and as *the* other acting upon and within herself. However that image was described or identified, it gave a double message, at once alluring and terrifying It demanded encounter and encounter demanded relationship; if not to the image itself, then to a third authority capable of meeting and withstanding it.

Here one has to speak of transference and, ultimately, of sacrifice. If, since she did not feel adequate to the confrontation, authority could not be called forth from within the woman herself, then it had to be temporarily vested in – i.e. 'transferred' to – someone else with whom she could trustingly relate until such time as she could find and integrate the capacity for authority which lay dormant within herself This explains Jen's phone call, and my questioning of whether I should take on Amanda. An example is Lisa's acceptance of Parson Peter to be mediator of her ritual. An illustration of the destructive consequence of someone's acquiescence and then refusal to fulfil transference responsibility is apparent in the case of Emily.

As the analyst involved, it became apparent to me that the analytic relationship, a relationship which demands to be no less human for being professional, no less involving of body or spirit for being psychological, was what prepared these women for their initiatory experiences and it did so to some extent consciously but also (importantly) unconsciously. Prior to the rites, I had to accept the transference of that which prevented the encounter – how often Jen and Emily reacted to me as the personification of that which forbade relationship! At the moment of ritual encounter, however, I became that which enabled relationship to the other because I, like Parson Peter, dared to go out and meet it; we had met before

Actually, this moment was psychologically prepared-for long ago, for each woman faced the event with a psychic pre-disposition formed in childhood. However, her preparation also included an important analytic component as well This came about as the result of her more recent experience of allowance, encouragement and non-betrayal of a primary but always temporary relationship attuned to her changing psychological conditions. When the moment came for encounter and transition from one way of being a woman to another, reliance upon memory of this analytic experience was of sustaining value. Strengthened by that, she had more than once sacrificed a previous condition and allowed herself to be involved in a new relationship with something that had previously appeared to be hostile, out-of-the-question and beyond reach because it was so threatening. And, as a consequence, she had been rewarded with renewal of authority in exchange for the risk of acknowledging that her present image was not adequate to her new condition.

In this way, rites of initiation serve to reverse the disintegrating effects of change and maturation One lets go of a past attachment to an inner condition, lets go reluctantly and not simply because it is past; but lets go to embrace a future which is more adequate than the present adjustment. Then one sees that the old condition which has been sacrificed is reincorporated in more complete and satisfying form. Similarly, one lets go of a much-loved but necessarily limited and temporary relationship for one which now matters more. And, although the beloved image of the past is gone, today's likeness more fully corresponds to deeply felt necessities. Understandably, Nicole cried for the loss of her doll's house and there were moments when, but for her vows, Jen would have pulled the rings from her ears. Yet, neither went back

The transference relationship, therefore, is a relationship to something other than a person, even though it is symbolised by a person. Ultimately, the ritualised relationship is to an image, that is, a metaphor for one's meaning and destiny. Psychological necessity evokes and ritual contains that image which initiates the foundation of a new way of being a person. A personal or transference relationship exists to serve that end. To be caught in a psychological world where nothing new can happen is unnatural and intolerable. Still, when something new happens, as new as shifting from undefined sexuality to womanhood, it is bewildering [11] One risks all that she has been, seemingly everything; a life is laid hold upon and the question posed of who or what will master it.

Initiation, rite and relationship go together. At times of initiation, even if not apparent, some sort of ritual is enacted and to be completed the enactment requires a relationship to someone real or fantasised who symbolises the mediatory function between the divine (initiator) and the human (person), enabling that which is spiritual (image) to become body (likeness). As Jung affirmed, we do not make images, rather, we are made by them.[12] And, when we lose the previous contact we enjoyed with them, as inevitably happens during transition, we have to rediscover a right relationship.[13]

The instigator of initiation and author of ritual can be seen either as the yearning of image to become likeness, which expresses an archetypal or religious point of view, or as the necessity for body to incorporate image which is a personal and maternal point of view. But, when directly confronted with the strong yearnings of image to become likeness, the yearning of a person is otherwise. He wants to stay as he is or, in any event, to transform (if at all) in his own time and upon his own terms. During this conflict of wills that ensues, the clash of moralities, ritual holds; a human relationship alone does not suffice. While symbol acts as go-between, ritual provides 'rite actions' *so that* symbolic communication can be established and maintained between an I and an 'Other' or, interpreted psychologically, between the likeness that I am and the image which I may to some extent become

Personhood (individuation or change of likeness) requires relatedness and companionship in order to mediate ritual encounter, however. Yet, at the same time, ritual lays hold upon relationship and utilises it in service to an unfolding that goes beyond the obvious banality of everyday and ordinary existence, i.e. to move in the direction of individual consciousness. 'Without the understanding of our case history as Arch-image of a divine mystery', states Father Thomas Carroll,

> we become once more prisoners of nature's mysteries and unchristened images. We live again in a sort of twilight timelessness in which past and future are vaguely present We see life from the other side of the tapestry, as it were, as so many unconnected, disconnected threads and it tells no story.[14]

One turns to the observance of rites when what confronts oneself is beyond the limits of belief and un-named. There is a prompting which makes this a natural and recurring need for a woman. But the gods served may be dark or light, life-enhancing or life-denying; for not all ritual ceremonies can be relied upon to carry the bride safely over the threshold, so to speak Ritual *per se* does not ensure a safe passage, but it does ensure that the passage is signified. Turner, the anthropologist, explains:

> What happens is partly a destruction of a previous being and partly a tempering of one's essence in order to prepare him to cope with his new responsibilities and restrain him in advance from abusing his new privileges Initiates have to be shown that in themselves they are clay or dust, mere matter, whose form is impressed upon them.[15]

In response to her encounter with mystery, a woman expresses the only individuality that is realisable for her and it is by this that her personhood will eventually be judged. A ritual fails only if mystery, elsewhere spoken of as the yearning of an image for realisation, fails to be registered psychologically. Otherwise, the rite impresses with a likeness called variously by many names· maturity, pathology, growth, accomplishment, deviancy, conversion, transformation, good behaviour. Yet, the person's own name for it must be *myself*.

CHAPTER 3

GROWING A WOMAN

The only status that is independently theirs, if status it be, is that
of woman
Lincoln, *Emerging from the Chrysalis*, Studies in Rituals of
Women's Initiation

'I feel so *guilty*', Amanda said, 'I never noticed my baby was dead and went on as if nothing had happened. Why didn't my body tell me or why couldn't I hear what it was saying?'

As members of certain tribes in Africa, women still go through extended formal rituals of initiation, both public and private. In the language of the Bemba tribe, these rituals are said to 'grow a woman', as if from a seed The rituals take place at puberty, at or about the time of first menstruation. In other words, the ceremonies are prepared to introduce a girl to the fundamental mystery of feminine body language. There was logic in Amanda's question. She had not yet learned to listen and translate the language of her body In the words of the Bemba, she was not 'grown' a woman.

With or without the benefit of ritual, a girl is naturally propelled toward womanhood at the onset of menstruation. For her, it signals an exit from childhood and an entry into adulthood It is a *rite de passage* between being born a woman and becoming a woman. Consciously or not, in the transitional space between two worlds, one that of the child and the other that of the grown-up, a girl/woman prepares to be the person she will be physically and also spiritually. Yet, however little or much she apprehends of her state of being at that time, the journey onward and into the next stage of life will be taken. She cannot linger on the threshold, her body assures that

In their book on menstruation, a major bestseller when it was published, Penelope Shuttle and Peter Redgrove referred to menstruation as *The Wise Wound*. Their interpretation of it was that the process which leads to scientific or artistic discovery involves a creative surrender and a rhythm learned by women from their menstrual cycle. 'We think that the physical process (makes) possible the mental one,' they write.[1]

Whereas I would shy away from the direct cause and effect relationship implied by such a statement, as a psychologist I acknowledge the inter-relationship of the two processes, one physical and the other mental or spiritual. And, as a woman at work among woman, I observe that we reach the spiritual by way of the material. These are two means of expression, each different. Neither is a substitute for the other, yet they appear to seek relationship with one another. And, it seems that, for a woman, insight and enlightenment in regard to the deepest issues of her life begin with the promptings of her own body. This appears to be true whether or not she has become conscious of body as 'beginning'.

When image becomes likeness, there is movement from *spiritus* to *anthropos*. Such an event must announce itself to and be received by a woman, be implanted physically before it can be made conscious. Menstruation, the first of her initiations, becomes a paradigm for all subsequent ones precisely because it 'happens' to her and is made apparent by evident body changes. Only later does meaning become manifest in such a way as to make individual sense of what is in the beginning a baffling and self-effacing event.

Listening to one's body language includes, but is more than, knowing when one is hungry, includes, but is more than, the awareness that one is ageing. It is connected with a spiritual-biological complex, otherwise called psychological which registers and expresses the totality of oneself as an individual, 'myself', 'all of me', a woman, body and soul, for it is in the psyche or soul that *spiritus* and *anthropos* unite.

Since both psychology and religion have addressed themselves to the inter-relatedness of body and spirit, the union can be explored from the perspective of either. Both traditions recognise that listening to one's body is part of listening to one's soul and vice versa. Body and soul are seen as inter-dependent, since body is that in which spirit humanly resides. When Amanda tried to locate the grave of her dead child, she searched for the body which her spirit neglected, longing to be reunited with the spirit which her body denied

The initiatory rites of the Bemba are there to assure that girls register the impact of a spiritual message from their bodies' changes. Rite is a means by way of which body meets and unites with meaning and is sanctified thereby, or, conversely, the place where spiritual commitment and belief are given body. But, to leave meaning separate and unrealised from body is to allow priority to unconsciousness, and the psychological task of 'growing a woman' will be incomplete.

Consciousness is sometimes equated with the discovery of meaning from unconsciousness. Therefore, contrary to the popular assumption that these are merely archaic remnants of ancient and pagan observances, initiation rites must be seen psychologically as attempts at consciousness-raising. The ceremonies are always impressive and memorable They fail only if they fail to impress a person in depth, and they succeed insofar as they provide for the emergence of a consciousness that has direct bearing upon the individuality of the one being initiated. But, if this connection is not registered, there remains a residue of something morbid and undisclosed which colours a woman's view of herself *and* her capability to relate to the opposite sex. She feels herself to be a victim and that same sense of victimhood will be projected on to the society and group into which she is inducted and granted status, i.e. the académe of Amanda.

The rites which have been reported here have an advantage for being spontaneous and self-devised. This gives them the authenticity and relevance of personal dreams – they speak from and to the person where she is, both collectively and individually. However, historically the conduct and content of such rituals have been protected and prescribed by society and, in the life experience of women today, this means that they bear vestiges of patriarchal dominance, distortion and overtone.

For example, it is easy to recognise patriarchal influences in the later-than-adolescence initiations of Nicole, Lisa, Emily and Amanda in particular; and, though perhaps in a less obvious way, patriarchal influences are evident in the initiation of Jen. This raises the question as to whether, for a woman, such influences can ever be eliminated or if the initiatory period is not itself a time of confrontation with that which is patriarchal, resulting, for better or for worse, in altered images and changed likenesses of both male and female within the same person. The corollary of this is that man as image of the 'not me' and *fully other* is seen as the instigator, perpetrator, impregnator and judge of events, real and/or imagined.

Let us turn to a review of rites connected and reported from a wide geographic area and belonging to somewhat different times. In and of themselves, they do not prove anything but mention of them may help us better to understand what is there enacted psychologically. Although the question of patriarchal influence was not explicit in Bruce Lincoln's anthropological study of women's initiation rituals, it is illuminating to note the titles given to the chapters written about traditional rites practised on five continents. In four instances the subtitles are 'The Marriage of Opposites', 'Becoming the Goddess', 'The Pattern of Time', and 'The Cosmic Tour'. The fifth chapter, a retrospective historical study of the Eleusinian Mysteries, is called 'The Rape of Persephone'.[2]

If we look at the titles for what they say symbolically, it is not merely the teachings of a particular psychological school that suggest we see them as emphasising *animus* or the image of man and masculinity that a woman carries within herself along with that of woman and femininity; male/female relationship appears to be what the rituals are about In other words, while being initiated, a woman discovers herself vis-à-vis a male dominant or aggressor who represents authority to her. What she realises of herself is in relation to what 'he' expects of her

Examining this more concretely, yet with symbolic and psychological overtones, in summary statements on the nature of woman's initiation, Lincoln describes the differing roles played by men and women in the initiation of young girls belonging to an Amazon Indian tribe. At one point in the ritual men impersonate demonic beings and assault the female initiand, accosting her with secret horns said to be demons' voices. The women act differently, however, dressing the maiden and adorning her, tapping her gently with leaves in token of their solidarity with her. They dance around her while she kneels during the night-long vigil before the day when she emerges from seclusion. But later, when her hair, symbolising her previous status and self-esteem, is plucked off, the first and last locks must be taken by her uncle, her father's brother, who stands over her.

'Thus, the women are identified with the initiand', writes Lincoln, 'they sit as she sits, forming a group, and all of them have suffered what she now suffers. In contrast, the man is the instigator of the ordeal, and the only one who can put it to an end. He is set above the initiand, physically as well as hierarchically. What he does, he does as an individual rather than as part of a group, and never will he experience the pain he inflicts '[3]

'Such distinctions, antagonisms, and tensions are always present in woman's initiations, where the initiand becomes to a certain extent the field on which the battle of the sexes is enacted,' he concludes [4] Reading this, 'How come and what for?' I asked myself, 'How come and what for did five others, individuals cut off from alternative sources of living ritual, devise for themselves rites that would re-enact a battle of the sexes? What were the implications to be derived from this?'

To help us consider the relevance of such a question for the individuals involved, we must refer again to Jung's empirical notion of *animus*.[5] He used this term to identify the image of man that a woman carries and which is determinative in her relations with members of the opposite sex. An image compounded of both body and spirit, corresponding equally well to a picture of her ideal man and to a statement of his expectations of her, it functions as consort and counterpart of herself as woman. Implanted as arch-image, this personalised form ripens into likeness as a consequence of her experience of maleness. It represents a force opposed to (but not necessarily in the sense of being 'in opposition to') her feminine being and, so, as 'the other', companion and awakener of her feminine potential, influences attitudes both to him and to herself.

However fully such a likeness ever corresponds to the authentic and universal image of man that co-exists and is co-eternal with that of woman depends to some extent upon the temperament of the receiving woman along with her experience This is a psychological figure, a personification, yet the one to whom she is wed in spirit and engaged in fantasy. 'Distinctions, antagonisms and tensions' with it are constantly operative It is not body, which *he* instinctively ravishes, nor mind, which *he* traditionally dominates, but psyche that is the field upon which the battle of the sexes is ultimately enacted.

Those who are acquainted with Jung's early writings on *animus* find here variations of his basic insights and dif-

ferentiations which have been made possible partly as a
result of more recent research and writing on the subject
of woman. There have also been shifts in the collective
consciousness of woman and dramatic changes have
taken place during the last few decades in regard to the
place of woman in society, her status and role. We now
speak openly and generally not only of consciousness but
also of 'woman's consciousness', her 'feminine self' and
'the feminine' with an awareness of her equality but difference that has been awakened by these changes.

Man's complementarity to woman is now expressed in
ways which would have been unacceptable only a few
years ago and before Emma Jung's intuitive foresights
about the psychological revolution facing woman once she
was able to control conception. We have also been reminded that the god-image, whether for a man or a
woman, is not always and only masculine, this, too, has a
counterpart and the counterpart is feminine. King and
Queen or Sol and Luna, as they were called by the
Alchemists, do in fact rule together in the human psyche,
however stormy or one-sided such regimes may become.

So the *animus* or image of man has to be recognised as
co-determinative in a woman's life, for it stands in relation
to her feminine image as that which she is not and cannot
become. To see it merely as confrontative, challenging or
aggressive ('instigator and perpetrator of the ordeal') is to
see it only in terms of patriarchal dominance or expressive
of only one end of an archetypal spectrum, as it were. It
can also be envisaged as complementary, inter-related, as
loving companion and partner, as well

When Jung speaks of *animus* as psychopompus or 'soul
guide', that may seem a somewhat old fashioned, quasi-
religious formulation. We must remind ourselves that he
is speaking about the psychological function of an image
that completes and complements the feminine psyche,
providing the stimulus for that which has not yet been
realised. Then, if we look at the individuality realised by a
person (called by Jung individuation) and see it as psyche

or soul's living expression, the fulfilment of the *animus* function is immediately apparent. Animus is that which furthers psyche's journey toward expression, embodiment or incarnation.

The image of man (animus) naturally cohabits with a woman's image of herself in her own psyche. The formation and transformation of psychic imagery and, ultimately, the change from image to likeness results from the union of these two. Their within-breeding accounts for either receptivity or defence against initiation and change as well as sexual involvement when a woman is 'grown'. But, consciousness of such a psychological *coniunctio* begins with rupture, a rupture made apparent at the time of first menstruation or initial intercourse, symbolising rupture from previous unconscious and incestuous attachments, and, that which ruptures, which is also what woman images as opposite and uncontrollable, is that which causes her to bleed

The blood she bleeds at the time of first menstruation and intercourse delineates a woman psychologically and symbolically Blood is a natural symbol of wound, sacrifice and martyrdom. It calls attention to her unconscious masculine image as well as to her feminine likeness. For, along with her woman's body, her ideal and image of man is also ruptured and must reform in response to what has now taken place Henceforth, she will express, assert, defend or repress not only her sexuality but a changed likeness to woman in response to an altered vision of man During the process of psychic transformation and integration that occurs with or without rite, inevitably she attempts to explain the mystery of her wound and thereafter she lives by the amended law that she finds and formulates. Jen wounded herself and said· '. . . I put holes in her ears and gave her gold rings to wear so that she'd remember she is a *woman for ever and ever*.' Whatever else they may have signified, the rings were a sign of her bonding to her new ideal and image.

He who causes her to bleed, the instigator, perpetrator

and rapist of woman's fantasy and consciousness, may be described by such terms as 'nothing but a male chauvinist pig', yet, secretly or otherwise, she may also see him in the guise of a divine Apollo In either instance, he has the status of a god, at least intrapsychically. He is both her lover and the meaning, the authority, for her loving. By way of his image she negotiates an implication formerly hidden but to be disclosed in her future life and behaviour He reveals to her the significance of her being. For a girl and in relation to meaning, father is no less important to her than mother who initiates her into life. It is he who initiates and accompanies her soul's transformation.[6]

What a woman is confronted with at that time of first menstruation and intercourse can be expressed as the loss of a former father/lover It is he who has provided the original law and established the order of her being. She is bereft of him and through ritual she must try to re-establish a relationship in a form superior to and transcending that which she has previously enjoyed. When a new influence breaks upon her and takes over (as Hades once broke upon the korē from out of the Underworld), the authority of the ruling father is either to be displaced or sacrificed to something more universal and transcendent.

It is the influence of the father, expressive of the primacy of the father/daughter bond, that determines a woman's attitude when introduced to objects that are symbolic of her liminal border condition at times of transition and it is by way of his doctrine, explicitly or implicitly, that awareness of their meaning is mediated and interpreted. Whatever is revealed to her at the time of initiation will be referred to him; he is her psychological reference point and spiritual rector. The lover she anticipates comes in his guise, psychologically. Initiation is the process of his more complete image being internalised.

In this regard, Amanda's father complex had been determinative in her life, conditioning her choice of profes-

sion, partner and her definition of personal boundary and
expectation. After the death of her child, how important it
was that her own father wept and she knew that he wept.
This opened the way for a new understanding of that
figure, personally *and* psychologically.

Rites provide a context that is more ample than the
ordinary personal one and, when needed, no conceptual
alternative, intellectual or scientific, suffices to take their
place. Among other things, they accord respect to mystery, the unknown and unknowable, giving it equal place
alongside the everyday and familiar. If someone has been
torn away from the familiar and is temporarily over-
powered by the *tremendum* and *numinosum* of an alien
force, it is the symbol and not the explanation that sustains her – sustains because it offers a possibility for questioning and reflects a core of mystery. Its very unknow-
ableness provides sanctuary from a fate that is overwhelming and appears to be inevitable

The as-yet-undisclosed extends hope of a solution other
than the one which seems inevitable at the time and one is
tempted to link with it by way of an imaginary relationship. Its amplitude and ambiguity embrace one; there
is space to withdraw into it; there is respect for the privacy, dignity and status of the person being initiated whose
only status at that moment is that of one who has been
deprived of status While in this condition, symbolic encounter affords someone not only anonymity but also a
certain freedom of movement and choice.

The words *outcast, abandoned, deprived* are strong words
and today's psychologists as well as social scientists often
choose to speak of rites of initiation in milder terms, de-
scribing them as devised to contain 'liminality', liminality
being the realm of rudimentary, archaic hypothesis. But
liminal or borderline states also have causal agents and are
always interpreted psychologically as having been insti-
gated by something or someone who triggers change
arbitrarily or advisedly dislodges and estranges a person
from the position which was formerly familiar, depend-

able and valued. If the shock of such deprivation is to be suffered and sustained, something or someone even stronger than the obvious agent has to be invoked.

When or if this happens, what a person then experiences is essentially religious His suffering is met and acknowledged by a higher, more inclusive presence and principle, even if this happens in the consulting room of a doctor or psychotherapist There was an eloquent though unconscious wisdom expressed by Parson Peter when he gave a sacred and sanctified name to that which had unwittingly taken possession of Lisa's body and had to be aborted.

Rituals of initiation mirror the psychology of change. There, symbolically, a woman is confronted both by herself and by her god The rites express, evoke and impart status to her vis-à-vis these two, her body-image and her god-image, at one and the same time. Her symbolic induction to a new status may be collectively prescribed and couched in conventional terms, but that which is demanded by the group impresses her only in as much or in so far as she is prepared to receive and accept collective tutelage. That is to say, she will be impressed in the degree and to the extent that she is open and ready for such induction. Yet, even when she rejects what is offered, draws back and withholds herself, a response is registered inwardly and will be reflected in her future attitudes.

Prescribed forms may not be made available to her by society at large, however, and she may seek the reassurances of private church rites supported by age-old dogma. Age lends these forms an aura of sanctification but, again, inner sanctification is admissible only with the permission of the spiritual rector and guide of a woman's psychological existence, namely, her animus Ultimately, it is a woman's own psyche or soul that the symbol must penetrate, impress and fertilise.

When we are confronted with unfathomable mystery, a religious attitude or sacred capacity is activated in any of

us. What is it that only a woman can receive during her
initiation and is connected with her particular mystery?
What is the nature of the sacred element or being to which
she is now introduced?

In answer to this, Mircea Eliade writes:

The woman receives the revelation of a reality that transcends her although she is a part of it. It is not the natural
phenomenon of giving birth that constitutes the mystery; it is the revelation of the feminine sacredness; that
is, of the mystic unity between life, woman, nature and
the divinity This revelation is of a transpersonal order,
for which reason it is expressed in symbols and actual-
ised in rites. The girl or the initiated woman becomes
conscious of a sanctity that emerges from the innermost
depths of her being, and this consciousness – obscure
though it may be – is experienced in symbols. It is in
"realising" and "living" this sacredness that the woman
finds the spiritual meaning of her own existence, she
feels that life is both *real* and sanctified, and that it is not
merely an endless series of blind, psycho-physiological
automatisms, useless and in the last reckoning absurd.'[7]

If, during the period of initiation, a girl responds only to
what pertains to sexuality in the symbolism of the rites,
she remains unconsciously wedded to the flesh with only
a limited awareness of the meaning of her body. If, on the
other hand, she is carried away by the spiritual impact of
the event, she may forget her body, so much so that she is
incapable of establishing a genuine relationship to it, physically or otherwise. Maturation, heralded by the sudden-
ness of the menarche, is an attempt to adjust and re-
establish herself, altered body and confronted spirit, a
new-born nature wedded to a re-formed law or standard

When such a marriage occurs, she is initiated into consciousness of her life purpose at the same time, what it
means to her to be a woman However well informed she
may have been about what was going to happen, at the
time of adolescence, a girl suffers the loss of a spiritual
principle capable of reconciling the life she has known

with its loss; speaking metaphorically, with its death and rebirth. She is now irrevocably rent from childhood; her psychological journey as an adult begins here Awareness must emerge from body, if it is conceived, its symbolism having been implanted in a bodily condition initially

As the enactment of tribal rites suggest, a woman's perception of the meaning of sacredness, as well as of sexuality, is impressed upon her by the *sacra* or sacred symbols with which she is presented, including the symbolic mediation she is offered as the *sacra* are revealed. The same could be said to be true whether the available context is religious or otherwise – i.e. a marriage rite or clandestine play, sacramental forms encountered in church, dream, analysis, on the marriage bed or if raped. Prior to impression, however, ego defences have to be broken through with sufficient strength to expose the naked psyche as well as the body to transformation. And, whenever this happens to a man or a woman, such an event is psychological, not mainly or principally physical or spiritual alone.

In his autobiography entitled *Memories, Dreams, Reflections* Jung speaks of his decision to become a psychiatrist as coincident with his realisation that 'this was the empirical field common to both biological and spiritual facts, which I had everywhere sought and nowhere found. Here at last was the place where the collision of nature and spirit became a reality '[8] Awareness of this combination not only led to his choice of psychiatry as his life's work but also led to the formulation of a psychotherapeutic method which would assure that attention was given to the healing of the split which automatically occurs, in man as well as woman, whenever shock, imbalance, break-up or loss of psychic equilibrium occur, a split between *physis* and *spiritus*

The symbol for shock, imbalance, break-up is being cast out, forced into seclusion or into the wilderness, plunged into darkness, exile, blindfolded. It is a symbolism offered in ritual and occurring in extant or spontaneous initiation

ceremonies wherever and whenever they occur. It takes
the form of withdrawal, solitude, disorientation and dis-
sociation and is mirrored clinically as depression We are
reminded here of the korē's trip to the Underworld, the
night-long ceremony of the Amazon Indian women, Emily's chronic depression, Amanda's tormented search
which was undertaken outwardly and pursued nightly in
her dreams. Here there is also an obvious connection with
old-fashioned attitudes towards sexuality itself, i e leave
it in the dark, leave it embodied. But the cover of night
is also symbolic of unconsciousness, which precedes the
coming of light or consciousness.

Thus far in this book when speaking of that which is
sacred to a person, it has been referred to simply as 'the
other' or a god-image. To many the sacred image is consciously admissible only when discussed as the image of
'an' other. Therefore, it would be easy to conclude that the
image which confronts woman is *only* an image of another
when she faces initiation I am convinced that such is not
the case, however. Every such encounter with a god-
image changes a woman's image of herself as woman and
her image of the one who serves *for her* as God. Put
another way, when the likeness of her self to her image of
woman is changed by the summons of her body, she is
likewise prompted to re-envisage the image of her god
Initiatory experiences result in a transformation of these
two images simultaneously: one sacred and spiritual, the
other material or profane.

> [Instinct] always brings in its train archetypal contents
> of a spiritual nature [writes Jung] which are at once its
> foundation and its limitation. An instinct is always in-
> evitably coupled with something like a philosophy of
> life, however archaic, unclear and hazy this may be . . .
> instinct cannot be freed without freeing the mind [9]

Application of these writings to our subject supports the
thesis that by way of her body a woman *instinctively* suffers the loss of a spiritual principle capable of reconciling
the life she has known with its loss Psychologically, this is

registered as a betrayal even though she may feel a heightened sense of elation in regard to a new-found sexuality and status. Metaphorically, her body exposes her to mystery, the mystery of herself, both woman and person. If she follows instinct alone, inasmuch as it is earthed in physical functions, she will submit to their command. If she dares to ponder the connection between her condition and its implication, however, she may be led to the discovery of her own conscious and individual law. She may then be able to use ritual as a symbolic expression of her need to relate to what she finds sacred and in time she may see her life as reflective of a natural spirituality.

Or, of course, the process of growing herself a woman may be interfered with, an interference akin to take over and rape from whatever source it comes, physical or spiritual (though the consequences are quite different). To become a woman is to expose oneself to that risk. The woman grown will be conscious of both body and spirit, not alone as outer realities but also for the way they affect her inner proportions, with a consciousness of soul without which she would be nothing but instinctive. Her awareness of inner proportion and balance becomes her law and gives her the authority with which she governs herself as a woman grown.

The paradigm of all her initiations will be the one she first experiences in adolescence. It is an end of childhood but now she becomes someone and something different, a woman. This initiation over-rides and challenges the adequacy and durability of her primary relationships, exposing her psychological formation and make-up. It sets the stage for and conditions her approach to man and influences her subsequent attitudes to herself as feminine as well as to the opposite sex. Subsequently the memory of this event is not just of a day, month or year but of a time, a time that subsumes and expresses the significance of her life.[10]

In that time she confronts three imageries, that of body, that of spirit and that of self or personhood. What begins as an end inevitably becomes a beginning for she has a chance to take possession in some degree of what has formerly possessed her. What she yields will become part of a more complete and adequate expression within herself. By the incorporation of spirit, she matures. To the extent that this is in relation to her unique possibilities, she will be satisfied as an individual. To the degree that it is not, she will undergo further initiations. And, if that which is actual and concrete remains disconnected, repressed and unconsecrated, the complete woman is stillborn.

With this in mind, let us return to the women who enacted initiation by way of analysis. What they revealed, clinically, were contrasting and incomplete images of themselves as women and also images that were incomplete and unsatisfactory to themselves either from the perspective of body *or* spirit. Consequently, analysis was used to redress that balance.

Nicole, who upon first appearance might have been assumed to be most in touch with her glamorous body, had never resolved the incestuous transference to her idealised father and was living in terms of *his* image of woman.[11] On the other hand, Jen unconsciously withheld her body from spiritual encounter; whereas Emily attempted to control her body by spiritual precept. Both of the latter had an animus problem; both suffered from a succession of bodily complaints The key for both was a return to the point of instinctive utterance that threw up symbols resulting in changed likeness and image of female and male, body and spirit. From then onward the personality was again free to act its age in relation to a contrasexual counterpart. A few months after the Christmas when she enacted her rite, Jen, a lapsed church-goer for whom English was not a first language, asked me if I could help her find a Bible in her mother-tongue One of the last problems remaining for Emily before she could get on with her dying was the problem of her sexual relationship to her husband.

Meaning can become a remote and esoteric, i.e totally spiritualised concept and the disembodiment of meaning is often a problem in analysis. If work is based on a medical or scientific model, the synthesis of *physis* and *spiritus* can be avoided. If, however, the conscious aim of therapy is to restore the balance of psychic (physical/spiritual) imagery, it involves paying attention to symbolism as dynamic, individual and medial. Here, awareness of the natural movement and direction of woman's initiation is necessary

Menstruation, marriage, pregnancy, menopause are all concerned with the making of meaning and not simply its expression. Change comes to a woman, is received and registered in body initially; only afterward does meaning disclose itself. What ritual reveals to her, consciously and unconsciously, is what has previously remained hidden but is now ready to be divulged. Afterward, she no longer knows in part or by hearsay but by way of her psyche or soul's own verification.

The place of openness and meeting where one is face to face with ultimate potential for good or evil is referred to as the heart of the mysteries and its time is eternal. Attaining the centre is an initiation and equivalent to a consecration [12] In ancient ceremonies only thereby and thereafter could one speak of transformation or renewal, whether of the individual or the group, since the group wherein the individual was finally accorded status was a group who had stood at that place and been present in that time. In that place and at that time, now as then, a woman discovers the right use of her changed body which is the same as to discover her law and its meaning The unconscious goal and intent of the summons to change is then met. She is grown.

CHAPTER 4

LOST VIRGINITY

It is woman's work to give attention to liminality, not just to the
liminality of being a woman
Henderson, *Thresholds of Initiation*

Thus far in this book woman has been spoken
of apart from man and her initiation has been
referred to almost as if it were her own exclusive
province which, of course, it is not Not only are
there initiation rites for men but, importantly,
men cannot simply administer rites for women. Un-
doubtedly men are also to some extent initiated alongside
and in relation to women at the same time. When we read,
'. . and never will the man experience the pain he inflicts',
we cannot help but fantasise the effect of the ceremony
upon him as well as upon her. And, for example, we ask
what may have been the effect upon Parson Peter, no less
than upon Lisa, when he named and committed to God's
keeping the soul of their out-of-wedlock child?

The extrapsychic effect of woman's initiation upon man
is not our subject or only inasmuch as a *woman* registers
what her 'becoming' does to him – father, friend, brother,
lover, husband, priest. But, the intrapsychic exchange is
of extreme importance. For, since both male and female

images are altered simultaneously at the time of initiation, not just her view of man is changed but a stream of consequences, psychological and otherwise, flows from such a shift. The way she behaves toward and with men alters.

The shift is from the image she has previously held and lived by. Now it is influenced and effected by he who officiates at the time of her initiation, as well. To identify the original image, we need to get as close as possible to the arch-image which has been manifested to her as girl-child and woman. The family member, analyst, elder, companion or priest, who presides at a time of her further initiation, will in all likelihood find projected on to him that self-same imagery But what we are speaking about here is something having to do with more than the obvious agent. Who or what initiates her is both more complex and more profound than can be observed and is immediately apparent

In traditional ceremonies, the role of the initiator was well and carefully defined Lisa, however, was initiated by the analytic process itself as well as in relation to myself and Parson Peter. Jen and Nicole more uniquely responded to an irruptive longing and urge which seemed to arise from deep within themselves and they became initiated when they could no longer bear to remain uninitiated. Emily and Amanda were impelled to seek, to ask, to enact, to dialogue and to discover their projections through the course of long encounters with psychic and bodily suffering.

For the most part, when ancient and present-day initiatory rituals have been reported, it has been supposed that the agent is simply the one who presides at the time when a new status is formally acknowledged. In the case of these women, however, the agent was described differently by initiates at different stages of their induction, even though the role and function of an agent did not change. At times it seemed that the one who presided was simply an 'other', masculine in character, who precipitated some sort of body/spirit encounter, at other times the function was fulfilled by the reconciling nature of the rite and its symbols; and at still other points, the agent became the inductor or companion (one who plays the part of therapist/priest) during enactment of the rite. These distinctions parallel movement through liminal space and time, from disorientation to integration, a progression mirrored by projection on to a dominant father figure, a mana personality acquainted with the symbolic objects, until that projection and transference are shifted to a renewed image within oneself. Finally the agent is at last consciously recognised as hierophant or 'he who makes the holy things apparent'.

Psychologically, the progression is from rupture and division of body and spirit to their eventual reunion in psyche/soul. It is obvious that during the interim period the so-called transcendent function bridges this split symbolically but that which impels the process can be identified no more accurately than an urge to grow and become other. Though it cannot (and I feel must not) be ignored as of deep psychological relevance (and we analysts have been neglectful in allowing the *telos* or goal to be cut off and assigned a category such as that of 'the religious factor'), persons must find and assign their own names to this agent. Agency, of necessity, conveys a sense of finality as well as cause.

'As we [see], final causes are brought to bear on the initiating, getting started side of things. They are the reasons why we do things, the goals toward which our behaviour is to be pointed,' affirms Rychlak, a contemporary humanistic psychologist, and he goes on to say: 'After a few years of trying to capture final-cause meanings in the language of responsivity, I realised that this was impossible and that another term was called for to oppose the meaning of "response" in descriptions of behaviour.'[1]

The term that Rychlak says that he stumbled upon was *telesponse*, a mental act in which the person takes on (predicates, premises) a meaningful item (image, precept, judgment) relating to a referent acting as a purpose for the

sake of which behaviour is intended. Telesponsive behaviour is therefore done 'for the sake of' grounds (purposes, reasons) rather than 'in response to' stimulation
or in-put promptings. It is teleogically oriented

This contribution seems relative to psychological process both in that it acknowledges the need for a purposive
rather than a purely descriptive concept and it enables the
analytic investigation of purpose. It is a theoretical extension rather than just a restatement of Jung's conceptual-
isation of the self with implications for understanding
therapeutic relationships and transference phenomena.
Though acknowledging the importance of previous root
causes of behaviour which have been the focus of both
psychoanalysis and scientifically oriented analytical
psychology, Rychlak's formulation in the end may offer a
means by way of which analysts and theologians along
with persons of other disciplines may investigate and compare similar happenings.

In order to explore further the applicability of telesponse
as a generative term for psychological behaviour during
initiation it may be helpful to look beyond the individual
case, however, and consider the myth which functions as
arch-image of feminine initiation For over a thousand
years the myth of the rape of Persephone served as the
basis for celebration of the Eleusinian Mysteries *where men
as well as women* were initiated by identical rites. Like all
myths, it is an archetypal metaphor for personal human
experience.

The myth deals with the breaking of a powerful mother–
daughter bond between Demeter, the earth goddess of
grain, and the korē, later to be called Persephone. The
bond is ruptured by the abduction of the korē by Hades,
Lord of the Underworld and brother of her father, Zeus.
Order under a new law is restored only after Demeter's
mourning, rage and vengeance have been spent and her
daughter Persephone is seasonally returned to the upper
world of consciousness Korē/Persephone's return brings
with it a renewal of fertility.

Regional and periodic inventions and additions to the myth have made of it a glistening web of complementary strands which lustrously illuminate the otherwise impenetrable and diffuse mass of psychic events surrounding feminine initiation. Although the heart or secret of the Mysteries was never revealed to the non-initiate, a stricture suggesting that the ineffable core not only must not but could not be disclosed to the non-initiated, there is no doubt that the progression of the rites followed the story symbolically [2]

To attempt a complete recapitulation of the myth is impossible; for, as symbol is a throwing together of two meanings, myth gives access to all relevant meanings. Myth is an arch-image revealed in word and story. The meaning one derives from it depends upon one's own personal orientation and development as an individual; while in contrast, the mythological figure acts from and within a universal context Therefore, the korē does not represent, she *is* all girls of initiatory age, and all that they can experience by way of initiation resonates in her myth.

We bring the case histories of our latter-day initiates to the myth for amplification, not for verification. None of the five initiates described in this book re-enacted the Eleusinian rites but each of the five was a true initiate in that her rites mirrored for the girl herself, whatever her chronological age, the next essential stage in maturation. And, had the rites not revealed to her an inexpressible core of mystery that pertained to more than her anatomical development and outward behaviour, they would not have been of such deep significance, bringing herself and her analyst to the threshold of psychological and religious investigation

How boys and men were initiated by participation into what were predominantly feminine mysteries is not our primary concern However, it is our concern that the initiation of girls and women was attendant upon a masculine component in the rites and here, again, we can use the myth as a symbolic reflection of the psychology of the

rite. Persephone, known initally as the korē, was a young
girl, a maiden on the verge of womanhood. The name
korē, meaning 'young girl of marriageable age', in the
Attic dialect, can be taken as synonymous with *parthenos*,
unmarried maiden, and the Hebrew *almah*, both terms
being commonly translated as virgin, though, as Layard
points out, the dividing line is not one having to do with
nature but with law.[3] The korē was unwedded.

As Layard also reminds us, Latin sources regularly refer
to the korē as *Virgo*. The oldest, most complete version of
the Persephone myth, the 'Homeric Hymn', calls the
maiden *thalere*, ripened. The assault of Hades is violent,
described by the Greek word *harpazein*, 'to seize, snatch,
carry off', translated into the Latin as *raptu*, meaning
'abduction, seizure, rape'. Korē is in the field, picking
flowers with her playmates. Beguiled by a narcissus
placed in her way by Gaia, the earth-mother, who acts on
instruction by Zeus, she is snatched away 'unwilling' and,
disconcerted, cries out not to her mother, Demeter, but to
her father, Zeus, for protection and help

From only this fragment we are able to see that the stage
has been set for a god-related, divinely intended incident,
Zeus being the greatest among the Olympiads and Demeter his wife/sister. They personify images of supreme
archetypal importance; the replay of their daughter's fate
will be inescapable in the lives of young women. The
korē's being seized and borne away to another world can
correspond to a girl's being wrenched out of childhood by
something that radically changes her condition and status
whether it be the sudden onset of menstruation, or initial
intercourse, or marriage

To the naturally intentioned incident of her deprivation
or abduction from her former life the telesponse of Korē is
to call out to her father. Her peers take up the cry as do,
according to other sources, Athene and Artemis, those
most unmarrying of goddesses. Zeus subdues the cries
with a clap of thunder and Korē, deceived by her father
(masculine) now turns unsuccessfully to her mother (feminine) for help before she is plunged into the mystery of

dark unconsciousness, isolation and solitude where she must submit to the difficult experience of transformation into womanhood.

There are correlations with the psychic drama re-enacted in the lives of my five analysands, though the myth must not be taken allegorically. Although married, perhaps Nicole was the most obvious korē or parthenos of the five, beguiled and entranced by a narcissistic attraction to her body, her self-image, her delicate beauty and a harmony unmolested by unpredictable and passionate demands Her benign father was a kindly, always to be trusted, somewhat saintly figure whose gracious influence pervaded her life and coloured her expectations for a future and husband. What her father had not fulfilled was the role commonly even if unconsciously assumed by the fathers of ancient Greece, illustrated in the myth by Zeus, the role of agent in the transfer of his daughter to the household of another man along with her transfer from the status of girl and daughter to that of woman and wife

There is no doubt but that the myth has an empirical fit but it is not a model and differs both from allegory and a telling of how it came to be. Therefore, the Eleusinian rites, though to some extent involving a re-enactment of original events, especially insofar as Demeter was concerned, could not be said to cause the transformation which came as a result. The ritual sacrifice, penance and progressions bore an acausal relation to a result made possible only if trustingly and, therefore, to some extent unconsciously observed by the initiate.

One consciously enters into a rite but ritual necessitates unconscious, i.e. symbolic exposure. The aim of the Eleusinian rites was not to implicate or educate but to permit embodiment or incarnation The same could be said of all ritual. Though the culmination and outcome of the ceremonies was spoken of by the Greeks as *theoria*, a visitation, representation or participation, no planned and conscious plot or model can ever completely exhaust or illumine the manner in which we come to know ourselves as ourselves At the climax of initiation, as at Eleusis, both disclosure (knowing ourselves) and insight (as to who we are) come together.[4] And here one is reminded, again, of Jen and Amanda especially.

That Korē's father-image was of Zeus and not just another of the gods or a mortal man is, of course, of significance when we look further at the psychology of the event Zeus was not, that is to say, *only* her father but a figure cast in the full proportion of father and father-image, personal and archetypal, humanly concerned and divinely wise It seems that he and Demeter had disagreed as to their daughter's fate. But Zeus was a no less devoted parent than his partner and, apparently with the child's best interest at heart, he eschewed a prolonged and static or regressive incestuous attachment, fulfilling parental desire/responsibility by handing her over to his dark brother who symbolised that which he was not and could never be for her, lover and husband. Simultaneously, she was confronted with the possibility of discovering the *telos* or meaning of her life, a possibility denied the so-human and lovable Emily so long as she lived in virginal dependence and inconsequence. By the painful loss of virginhood, Korē and her modern counterpart discovered womanhood Correspondingly, their images of man, having been shattered by betrayal, reconstellated.

Many women refer to times of seclusion and the depression which is a prelude to insight as 'being in the underworld'. In the early days of Jungian psychology there was frequent reference to being 'taken into the belly of the whale' at such times. Another metaphor, this time with religious connotations, is 'the dark night of the soul'.

But that which distinguishes initiatory solitude for a woman is the ritual task she performs consciously and unconsciously during seclusion, the task of reconciling two conflicting images, one that of a known father, real or imagined, with this 'other' man, Hades/Zeus combined, he who rends the earth beneath her feet and he who, ignoring her cries, lets it happen. When Hades appears in life as seducer or husband, he invades the woman's body

itself, claiming invasion as his right. This may appear to be
a purely sexual and one-off experience but it has psychological repercussions. Whenever and wherever such a take-
over occurs, a woman is startled, alone and at a loss to
explain herself to herself until she is able to reflect and find
her own word to clarify the logic of such an event.

It has become commonplace to speak of post-natal
depression and the 'baby blues' to describe the reactions of
women after they have given birth and are on the
threshold of a new status, that of mother. From conversations with many women, I am also aware that unvoiced
feelings about post-marital depression, 'brides blues' – connected with their coming to terms with the status of wife –
likewise affect attitudes towards themselves and marriage
for years to come, including attitudes fundamental to their
further physical and spiritual transformations. Non-
recognition of such depressive fantasies impedes sexual
expression and to some extent explains gender inhibi-
tions.

Unless times of liminality are accorded a place in proportion to their importance in the lives of women so that
what they symbolise is worked through in depth and with
respect for whatever is believed to counsel such changes,
unresolved difficulties re-assert themselves from the confines of unconscious shadow. The need to accord space,
time and place for liminal feeling and ritual enactment was
largely ignored in Western society for centuries. Now this
need once again commands attention. We see it reflected
in the increased demand for analysis. It shows itself in the
resurgence of interest in such phenomena as the 'Black
Virgin' and the observance of cult rites We hear it in the
outcry for changes in women's rights and status.

What takes place in the dark phase of liminality is a
process of breaking down, differentiation and purification
of one's attitudes in the interest of 'making whole' one's
meaning, purpose and sense of relatedness once again. At
that time, metaphorically speaking, the as-yet-unmarried
prepares for marriage: reality with ideal, changed physique

with new-body image, altered awareness with spiritual understanding, the unknown with the consciously known, mystery with matching Mystery, the personal with the Universal To refer to this period of change in the over-used and commonplace terms employed by media reporting avoids recognition of the necessity for privacy and seclusion, the part played by the unconscious at times of transition and the psychic demand that a place be given to consideration of the transcendent, referred to here as the god-image or Mystery. Sexuality is more than an aspect of our reality, it provides the vital energy of which physical expression is essential but only a part of the whole. Sexuality needs to be seen also as a medium that puts us in touch with other realities and other selves than that of the enraptured lover alone.

A woman's instinctive pursuit during liminal seclusion is to search for a reunion as herself, body and soul. There is an evident parallel between an assertion of Jung's and that of someone writing about this from a theological point of view Jung writes· ' . . just as the material of the body that is ready for life has need of the psyche in order to be capable of life, so the psyche presupposes the living body in order that its images may live.'[5] A parallel statement would be· ' . we are an incarnate spirit, and the plenitude of man does not lie in his spirit or in his soul, but in spirit-soul together with his body.'[6] Continuing with another writer, a theological essayist, we read: 'Man's reality is an embodied reality, and so much so is this the case that for him to think or attempt to act as though he possesses a soul apart from a body is to cripple its nature at its roots.'[7]

For many women alive today it is 'men' who take the full projection for crippling their nature at its roots and for some, like Emily, this may appear to be the truth of the matter; true, that is, to her psychological case history. But the psychology of woman also depends upon man for its completion. Even when there is a 'missing' man, he will be there *in substitutio*, for it is impossible for her to realise herself without a concept of an 'other' as partner and counterpart. Analysis can be the process of becoming aware of those images that dominate our lives, their sources, their distortions, their inadequacies – in short, their darkness as well as their light. Initiation, however, is the process of suffering change in that imagery, which means bringing to consciousness something of what has formerly been undisclosed.

There is risk in letting go to liminality, though; witness the korē shock and disorientation when deprived of her narcissistic attachment to an unshadowed and unchanging existence Can a way back be found to the ground of her reality? To assure that she lets go, Zeus, the Almighty, ordains that his daughter is transported from her former life but her fondness for it, the warm fertility of her own beginning, assures that she will return seasonally, though no longer as Korē; now as Persephone. The girl becomes an individual and her own name is bestowed on her after she has been initiated in the Underworld and made aware of herself as woman, having finally sacrificed her unmarried status. '(Now) the lost paradise is no longer *in potentia*,' comments Corbin. 'The potential will be born (or reborn) from the act, from the test of initiatory faith which will allow the divine incarnation to individuate as the human creature, individuality being equated with becoming conscious of one's own image (body) and idea (spirit) of the divine.'[8]

Yet, an open attitude to the hours of estrangement, seclusion and struggle with the irrational is not to be equated with 'abdication to the absurd'.[9] Neither should it be summarised simply as death and rebirth, bypassing the implications of its unconscious religious imagery. The initiatory test or heroic feat made so much of in the early literature of analytical psychology is, however, a male derivative and refers to whether and how a boy will embody a spiritual principle. The test for a girl is whether she can discover and relate to a spiritual principle already implanted symbolically in her own body. And, for either,

what initiates recovery from one condition carries in
embryo the form of a new condition to be re-initiated at a
later stage in the time of another of life's seasons.

By virtue of being female, a girl is exposed to two wis-
doms, one imprisoned in matter and the other conveyed
by matter, the first relatively still (her own space), the
other moving (representing spiritual necessity or time). To
one she is bonded; to the other she actively weds. Here is
a timely warning for feminists and patriarchs alike. For it
is not society, any more than the personal father or husband *per se* who is the agent of initiation for a female
daughter or bride although each plays a part, knowingly
and unknowingly Initiation as a transmutation of psychological or sacred imagery depends upon several elements,
her nature, the image of herself as woman in relationship
to man which has been aroused within a girl during pre-
adolescent years, her response to what is offered as symbolic induction and the figure, real or imagined, who
mediates the induction.

Further analytic or psychological analogies become evident when placed alongside the myth:
' . . along with my virginity', the korē laments, 'The
sky is taken from me;
My purity is snatched away with the light and I must
depart from earth.'
The black Underworld is the locus of liminal existence.
Unable ever to return as a child to her mother, but yearning for that former mode of being which has provided her
with the nurturing warmth of 'mother', a girl is bereft.
Rupture induced by an other, real or projected, alienates,
injures and, so, betrays the logos upon which she has
come to depend, whether that logos has been consciously
interpreted or simply assumed by way of a father's discipline, society's precepts or the dogma of a religious institution. To reinstate herself, she must change, if only to
accept change. This is the inexorable demand made by her
body. In some manner, she must re-establish relatedness
to her femininity which is so different from that to which

she had grown accustomed and to a masculine/spiritual authority co-existing in relation to that femininity. Transformation is not sought as desirable in and of itself; it is a command of her being

In liminality where she is exposed to symbols mysteriously related to her condition, shifts occur, shifts between a girl's image and likeness to woman; so, also, between the image of her being of which she is conscious and the image-in-potential of herself as individual of which she is still unconscious Mother cannot teach her girl child to be a woman; she can only expose her to the necessity of being a woman. For this she prepares her by giving her birth, conveying to her an attitude loving or otherwise about being a woman and lamenting *with* her, but not *as* her, the abduction she suffers by intervention of the fate not intended by herself but decreed through the counsel of Zeus. (Here one is reminded of the symbolic all-night vigil of the Amazon women – attending until the dawn of consciousness.) The mother knows that a time of darkness is essential, if a daughter is to become a woman 'Thus', Lincoln remarks, 'when Demeter mourns the loss of her daughter, she simultaneously celebrates her transformation.'[10]

Through suffering her own solitude, the korē becomes koran and 'like unto a woman'; yet, also, 'like unto herself' as well. Her conscious image of man is changed not just by her abduction and alienation which symbolise a loss of previous status but also partly by the intervention of a father who first instigates but later calls a halt to a liminal and outcast existence. For, according to the myth, Zeus eventually sends Hermes as messenger to intervene with the dark and sinister god, Hades, who has become his daughter's husband. Thus, Korē's return is enabled.

In ancient Greece Hermes is known as the bringer of dreams. He acts as intercessor, messenger of the gods and agent of change. He is a go-between and, since the traffic is two-way, one must assume there is benefit in or to both realms. Himself a liminal figure, part human and become

god, Hermes moves and communicates between worlds;
Olympus, earth, the Underworld or realm of death, and
plays with or at the delivery of symbols as well as the
matching of symbols, irrational to rational and vice versa.
In terms of analytical psychology, he personifies the transcendent function of the psyche This is the symbol-
making-function and its messages are of immediate and
long-range import, relative to cause and to purpose.

When the work of analysis touches upon Mystery, we
have need of contact with and respect for the eternality of
events which are mythically replayed – replayed by
women not as Korē but as likeness to her, with her image,
and by men in response to her and to that image In this
connection, since the rites celebrated at Eleusis initiated
men as well as women, they have added significance for
us. The assumption that joint initiation was evidence of a
lingering matriarchal influence is probably not true, or, at
least, it is not particularly relevant psychologically. For,
whatever the conduct of the rites may have been, there is
reason to believe that it was the same for both men and
women and we know that the climax was in the nature of
a revelation of equal but different importance to both sexes
and regarded as of sacred and final or purposive content.

Only a unifying principle or an image that transcends
physical sexuality itself could provide the context for this
The *visio beatifica* must have been of something which
embodied the principle of one's self-manifestation, masculine *or* feminine, and formed the basis of a particular
relationship between that image and the infinite. It was an
image that revealed the principle of the archetype and, at
the same time, laid the foundation for a personal relationship to that principle.

To return to the consulting room of the analyst or,
perhaps, more directly to the psychic location of woman
as initiate, in liminality she confronts the ugly spectacle of
herself as inadequate and besieged by masculine and feminine voices simultaneously By nature she is feminine and
her unconscious reference is mother; yet, her protector/

attacker is masculine and his counter-part is father. Because of her loss of steadfast and dependable references at this time, priority of position and influence is lodged in the *sacra* or symbols which she is shown, although she may not allow them the full significance they can convey if her consciousness has been impaired by too close or too traumatic a bond with her personal mother/woman or father/man.

What a woman feels in such a bewildering place and at such a difficult time, as Emily did at an advanced age, is expressed in words such as, '. . . but my mother never mentioned these things' or 'surely those men could have seen what was happening'. 'But, then', she implores, 'if they knew what it was all about, why didn't they *help* me? Why didn't they *do* something about it?'

When the initiator is an actual man, as he is for a woman when she becomes his bride, the intruder and rapist is certainly not just a projection of a spirit being. He is also a man in the flesh and what he does, he does partly by way of the flesh. Thus, he represents both man acting in a man's body but also for the body of men The distinction which women today feel and voice, that of estrangement from a male dominated society, could herald the onset of a collective initiation and might lead to a new stage of collective maturation *but only* if the full implications of sexual roles and rape (not alone the rape of one's rights) is allowed to penetrate psychological awareness. This would have the possibility of connecting us with a new awareness of sexual difference and would be essential in creating an integrity from schism. But have we the trust, both men and women, to withstand societal liminality without disintegration and pursue consciousness rather than reparation for what has wounded us?

We must assume that all-powerful Zeus did not instigate the rape of his daughter by his dark brother in response to whim but that it was, in a real sense, a telesponse in keeping with an ultimate and profound necessity. Why, otherwise, would he have stood aside? As a result, both he as father and his daughter sacrificed a relationship which had formerly been pleasurable to them. He forewent any desire to keep her, a prize for his own delight alone, while she was forced to surrender hope that he could be counted upon to stand by her at all cost or that their relationship would endure without change forever.

From the foregoing, we may presume that what a man discovers during an initiatory period is a testing and application of his natural logos in relation to body and what a woman discovers is an application of her body in relation to its ultimate purpose But the quest of discovery is not asked of her solely in response to the command of any man or of society, it is a requirement of her own soul. Hypothetically, does this not suggest the importance of the Eleusinian Mysteries of both men and women? Were they not, perhaps, an introduction to woman's mystery as essential to the consciousness of both sexes? It might not be too much to expect of clever, far-sighted Zeus that he lay the trap for an event of such consequence. Whatever happened, however, was by the agency of the korē herself, initiated by the wisdom of Zeus and it was more than of mother/daughter significance, symbolised ultimately by a seed of pomegranate rather than the grain associated with the fertility of Demeter and the material world.

Kerényi's treatment of the myth convinces me, as did the experience of the five women with whom I worked, that whatever happens that can rightly be called initiation, which is finally the same as a confrontation with Mystery, cannot be apprehended from a cause and effect point of view alone and this is the limitation of much psychological, medical or scientific endeavour. It speaks of a sequence in linear progression or builds from known relationships a model. Yet, the sequence of a profoundly transfigurative (i e. psychological, religious or imagistic) experience, an experience of Mystery, is not linear, though neither is it circular in the sense that it *achieves* a centre [11]

Complete apprehension of an image does not occur in

an absolute sense. Conforming by likeness cannot be compared to the completion of a jigsaw puzzle. What the initiate 'sees' is reflective of and elucidates all else that has formerly been seen, hence something expressed psychologically as formerly repressed or unremembered by the initiand. At the same time, it also includes what has not previously been seen in a form individually apprehensible. But it is never all; i.e. all that may be apprehended at some future time, if one is ready.

Perhaps it is appropriate to describe initiatory seeing as in a better light, as if the sun has at last come out from beneath a cloud, revealing hitherto obscured aspects of a scene, both features that one has many times observed and also basic contours that have escaped one's previous notice That is to say, one sees subjectively and, yet, with a new degree of objectivity. And, also, one sees with a new comprehension of totality made possible by the conjunction of inner vision or 'inscape' along with outer vision or 'landscape'.

This way of seeing, coming at the climax of initiation and expressed in words used to describe the Eleusinian experience, is 'a vision of completeness'. It confers upon the see-er a sense of participation in the original myth: the story is no longer repeated as a dry allegory but sensed to be capable of infinite variation and repeated transmutations. Likewise, the *visio beatifica* has an application to personal experience.

Man is psychologically energised not by model but by myth, dream and parable which is the same as admitting that his most basic reference point is to something mysterious, archetypal and religious rather than cognitive and limited by his own humanity and human perception. His life is not a discovery of how better to be a man or woman but an *imitatio dei* and by initiation he is introduced to aspects of his original myth of possibility. By contrast, models are manmade and can only be constructed from the already seen and known. There are no metaphorical models, metaphor and myth inhere to mystery. There is al-

ways something implied but inexpressible in exact terms;
it remains inconclusive, descriptive and related but indis-
tinct.

The central implication of this mythic tragedy, that Korē
was inevitably torn from her former community, is that a
maiden/woman had to suffer a sacrificial death and go into
the Underworld not only for her own sake but also for that
of the very community from which she was wrenched. It
is this suggestion which retrieves the tale from tragic and
punitive consequence. The father, sensing the error of
limitation in arrogating to himself the role of seducer and
personal initiator, takes care to see that his place is taken
by his shadow brother, Hades, god of the Underworld
So, Korē is not merely taken hostage by Hades; she is
transported to the realm of subterranean fertility, taking
an erstwhile death upon himself in order that therefrom
benefits will flow for herself personally and for all people.
A break is made with omnipotent and idealised fantasy so
that a union can be established with the sources of eternal
life

This is the outcome imputed to these mysteries by
Kerényi in his *Hermeneutical Essay on the Mysteries*. In the
course of his work as an anthropologist and analyst, John
Layard also concludes that '. . the incest taboo is the
exile which cuts mankind off from the object of his most
intense desire in order that, through exile from it in the
flesh, he may re-discover it in the spirit.'[12] Such a view is
consistent with Jung's interpretation of the function of
incestuous fantasy as part of psychological process.[13] 'It
was only the power of the "incest prohibition" that created the self-conscious individual, who before had been
mindlessly one with the tribe; and it was only then that
the idea of the final death of the individual became
possible.'[14] Death was not realised for Korē in the Underworld; death would have been an extension of her unmolested and paradisal life as a child on earth

Pursuing the theme further in relation to our myth,
what besides abduction, seclusion in darkness and sub-

mission serves to transform the virgin so that the anguished korē becomes Koran, Persephone, 'grown' a woman? Is it the remonstrations of her mother, Dementer, who goes into mourning, vengefully withholds fertility from the fields, zealously sets torches aflame and by the blazing light of whatever consciousness she can command searches out the dark corners of the world for evidence of her lost daughter who has been snatched from the confines of her maternal care? Figuratively speaking, such hysterical behaviour was not unlike Jen's irate and panicked bewilderment at her loss of a young boy's persona during analysis, before and until she could acknowledge that 'she' existed, even though separated from her, and could believe that even if cut off from all that she had ever longed 'her' to be, 'she' was, nevertheless, worthy of notice and adornment.

Later in the story of Korē/Persephone, what is the significance of Demeter's attempt to immortalise the infant son of those in whose house the ridiculous and bawdy behaviour of a servant girl first causes her to laugh after losing her daughter? Here is a mythologem reminiscent of Lisa's initially jocular but superior attitude to the attentions of Parson Peter. But, all the same, what is attempted by Demeter is the negative counterpart of what takes place in the Underworld at the behest of Zeus Is it, perhaps, the power of his will alone that must be broken so that he finally relents, returning the korē as koran to the upper world and that world to fertility?

These suppositions, though part of the fabric of the myth, are too limited as explanations of the cosmic significance of the eventual transformation of Korē/Persephone, making it synonymous with the gift of initiation into infinite and ultimate Mystery. This is transacted by Hades himself, by his offering to his bride and by her eating 'only a single sweet seed of the pomegranate, a seed so small that she barely noticed'. It is after the eating of the seed given her by the god of the unconscious Underworld that she transforms After this, nothing done by her mother, Demeter, or her father Zeus, can ever make her the same again. [15]

As Kerényi carefully points out, the eating of the seed is
not the secret of the Mysteries; else it would not have been
spoken of in public. But the seed *symbolises* what was
ingested and integrated that became the agent of transformation and exposed the heart or meaning of the Mysteries Here fact helps little; historical imagination and
amplification help more.

In later times the pomegranate was known as the fruit of
bloody death and dedicated to Hades. Greek references to
it range from suppositions that it symbolised fertility by its
abundance of seeds (thereby suggesting a likeness and
bonding between Persephone and her mother as goddess
of grain) to earlier legendary suppositions whereby it was
linked with the rites of Attis whose myth symbolises the
death and survival of vegetation. When Agdistis, the bi-
sexual primordial form of the Great Goddess, was emascu-
lated, the pomegranate tree sprouted from the blood that
flowed and the Great Goddess, now Great Mother, conceived by eating the fruit. So it has to do with differentiation of a previously unconscious union and suggests the
ripening of femininity. Can it be the fruit of woman's
realising herself?

When a Greek villager greets his new bride with the gift
of a pomegranate today, he may, like the farmer who
breaks the fruit on his ploughshare, see no more in the
gesture than a token of his wish for abundance. But the
desire for conception should not be confused with hope
for fertility and such practices may relate to this even older
rite. The pomegranate seed identifies Korē with the
Underworld as the Underworld was the home of the dead
and Hades, god of the dead, was represented with a
pomegranate in his hand. An archaic image of Athene
Nike (like Artemis, ever korē) shows Athene in her temple
on the Acropolis holding a pomegranate in her right hand,
while in her left is a helmet, symbol of worldly prowess,
might and government. Can we not suppose that the
pomegranate as emblem of the Underworld here signifies
the possibility of joining two realms, one plant-like and

bodily, the other spiritual? For the Greeks, the location of the eternal abode of soul and spirit was below the earth, not above it The world was the place of conscious involvement and action, the Underworld the place of unconscious consequence.

We are told by Proklos, the neo-Platonist, that 'the great and ineffable secret of the Eleusinian Mysteries resided ultimately in the cry of "Hye; kye!",' the mystical incantation which accompanied the pouring of sacred libations into the earth following the Mystery Night. '*Hye*, meaning flow; *Kye* meaning conceive.'[16] A connection with menstruation and fertility is obvious but to leave it at this is to minimise the high point of the initiation ritual which was a direct experience of divine imagery What Korē is given is a seed which enables her to incorporate this mystery. It is a pledge, not of productivity alone but also of immortality

The seed is not the vision, yet it prepares for the ultimate vision, only after eating it can Korē, the initiate, see herself in the vision. Having swallowed it, she looks, as it were, into the abyss of the seed itself and there beholds the feminine source of life as the source of life common to all men and women because it implies death to the body and rebirth in the spirit. [17]

At the epiphany of the mystery rites, people saw a vision of that which she, Korē, also 'saw' by taking into her body the seed of pomegranate which would heal the split caused by the experience of being lost to life and the necessity of finding it again in a new form. They saw this with eyes already opened by things previously revealed. With the seed she ingested the awareness that she herself had become as a seed, a symbol of renewal and resurrection So, at the climax of the Mysteries, she who was Queen of the Dead now gives birth to light. 'It is attested that Persephone was looked upon as the goddess of fire . . (and) the reason for this, evident at Eleusis, was that through her power the evil element was transformed into a kindly one.'[18]

The korē is symbolic of undivided existence, an exist-

ence unaware of its duality The splitting of the seed
makes possible material increase, fertility, but the meaning of the seed is resurrection. Envisioning this, which
was the telos or purpose of induction into the Eleusinian
Mysteries, has to do neither with the imparting of knowledge nor the formation of character. It is a manifestation
of the supreme being which pierces through the sign.[19]
Such a vision of the ultimate can only be expressed by
imagery and, therefore, is comprehensible to the soul
rather than to the mind. Seeing it, initiation is completed.

The psychological counterpart of the culmination of an
initiatory process is awareness of transformation, of having been transformed. One now sees what one didn't see
before Jen, for example, sees through Jen's eyes, not the
eyes either of a young boy or of a fantasised 'her'. Emily,
who has spent a lifetime as Korē, struggles to see with the
eyes of Persephone on the threshold of death Eyes
opened, Lisa discerns a path from the cemetery to the
altar And each of these women sees and accepts that the
principle of her life may be more surprisingly but wisely
counselled and regenerative than she could formerly have
recognised or comprehended.

But, if seeing this brings a certain degree of confidence
and hope along with the risk of psychic inflation, initiation
also brings with it suffering and, as a result of suffering,
the possibility of a sense of proportion, humility and ear-
thiness, as well For, when initiation is successfully completed, each is one with her own mode of being, her own
form of existence. Image and likeness of 'myself' and 'a
woman' have been reunited and form a new balance.

CHAPTER 5

ENDANGERED DAUGHTER

> But can the way to the lost paradise of love ever be found again if
> the passage from the sensible to the spiritual is definitely
> destroyed?
> Corbin, *La Sophia Eternelle*

Asymbolic relationship is not one confined to discussion of symbol; it is one which offers the matching side of the *symbolon*, completes the tally and hence, reveals its meaning. The partner of woman is man, without him, her *symbolon* is incompleted. Each of her major transitions is a marriage to a different, formerly alien or absent psychological partner. Metaphorically speaking, whenever she finds herself in need of renewal, she approaches the altar yet again, seeking a renewed relationship with the image of the one she identifies as father/lover/husband. This has to happen before the body/soul split that she suffers can be healed.

At that time, a profound responsibility is placed upon the one she meets by choice or by chance. Whoever he is, she inevitably sees him in the likeness of bridegroom. Whether ordained and appointed for his task or spontaneously and personally chosen, he must be dedicated to consciousness for this is a treacherous but, in some measure, also a sacred undertaking At least, it opens the way for a woman's experience of the sacred and the work is not to save or to cure but to wisely accompany her on a natural journey toward an as-yet-to-be recognised destination. The one who undertakes such a journey with a map and a feeling of sure knowledge of the goal inevitably misleads.

We who find ourselves in the position of companions – lovers, family members, priests or professional psychologists – are supported by the deep sense of ritual requirement that is inherent in those we accompany and in ourselves as human beings Ritual, as we know, is both sequential and mythic, so that one emerges from rite with a sense of having been altered or transformed by exposure to an imagery of cosmic proportion yet by way of a metaphor that is personally relevant. Importantly, only a mythic and ritualised encounter is capable of producing this dual effect.

Precisely at this point, however, all systems of hermeneutics. philosophical, scientific or otherwise, become inadequate. The transition from the recognition of a universally applicable idea to an awareness of life as living myth separates the intellectual from the noetic, the artistic, or the authentically religious and psychological whereby we apprehend meaning by means of dream, metaphor, parable, symbol and image. Interpretation, investigation, learning or dramatic replay may enhance our understanding but mystery alone, a sense of possibility for infinite particularisation, initiates. Yet, encounter with mystery is dangerous; both the guide and the one whom he guides can lose a sense of proportion.

An awareness of mystery begins with the recognition that we are more and other than we consciously appear to be But, someone who is pathologically enveloped by mystery will see himself *as* the mystery and the all important distinction between an *I* in relation to a *Thou* is obliterated This results in hybris, an identification with the archetype of the other or god-potential. The opposite may happen as well, of course; a person may feel belittled or helplessly 'nothing but' small and inadequate. It behoves the initiator, presumably the wiser or at least the more conscious of the two, to leave a place for recognition of difference between an I and an Other-than-I and approach mystery with humility and respect Otherwise the soul is endangered.

Jung reached an empirical conclusion, which he often referred to, that he had to treat people *as if* they had a god-image even though he was at pains to say that this was not the same as treating the god-image itself.[1] Treating the man-image of woman presents us with difficult problems since this man-image at times and of necessity coalesces with the god-image. At any rate, the god-image assumes the place of a ruling father in the destiny of woman. Man is, in fact, the personification of woman's Other-than-I, her companion and spouse in the space which unites body and spirit worlds – person, symbol and, at times, endowed with attributes which belong to her God.

When in the destiny of a woman that which functions to link her with her god-image becomes that image, she is confronted by a ruling father in the personality whose presence is numinous, overpowering and dominating. Subject to his law and circumscribed by his meaning, what she conceives is at his behest, whether he himself impregnates or, like Zeus, insists that another do so. The tempering of her god- and father-image, which functions as animus in psyche, to a large extent determines her freedom to express her natural womanhood.

Jung concluded that a woman's man-image, her animus, linked her with her god-image but he also said that in its highest form, the animus functions as the archetype of meaning, which is the same as saying it is a god-image. The two parts of this statement must be seen as complementary. Linkage implies a relationship but meaning is that which flows (is conceived) from a relationship.

Today we observe that the patriarchal image is aggressively apparent in modern feminism despite an avowed purpose which is to break the rule of the patriarchy. Although modern feminists no longer go forward on behalf of their god-the-father, nonetheless, as was true of Athene, the advance is made under his aegis and in obedience to a projected man-image that has significantly shaped feminine expectation and belief. When this happens, an outcry that purports to be an escape from the patriarch resounds with his voice and makes use of his words, having been incestuously conceived within the confines of an unchanging image limited by space and time. It speaks of a powerful psychological projection not yet integrated

Here, however, I am concerned with the way in which a more distant personal father, someone who, like the father of Jen, opts out of involvement with his daughter I am not only mindful of the father who remains unconscious of the effect of his influence upon his daughter but also of the father who for whatever reason abdicates incest responsibility, bypasses encounter with mystery and, hence, leaves her discovery of meaning to chance. Thereby he neglects his function as the one who links his girl child with her god-image, but, nevertheless, knowingly or unknowingly, he takes control of her destiny.

Paradoxically, the fathers of both Nicole and Emily did precisely this though of the five fathers, all active in their daughters' lives, these men probably paid most attention to the inculcation of what they supposed were meaningful values; cultural, religious and otherwise. Where they proved less than adequate, psychologically, was by never counselling or acknowledging the necessity for a disruption of an infantile and harmonious relationship with their daughters. They seemed to lack the courage to test whether such a disruption would lead to renewal and, as a consequence, they bound their daughters to their own beliefs by devotion and obedience There was no space for breakthrough to awareness of a more significant or personally satisfying standard Psychologically, the girls were placed in a double bind; they felt naturally impelled to disobey, say goodbye and move on; yet, at the same time, they were enjoined to stay ever korē and on the threshold of becoming women.

We must realise that whatever adjectives we employ to describe such fathers; whether we label them strong, stalwart, idealistic and protective, or limited, possessive, short-sighted and weak, each of our words supports a context of meaning to which we ascribe. It is only if we can free ourselves sufficiently from such categories that we are able to observe that a father's attentions, extrapsychic and intrapsychic, act symbolically and do so by his holding steadfastly (as Zeus held) or otherwise to the man's fragment of his daughter's *symbolon*. So doing, a father not only presents the symbol but at times becomes the symbol by way of his relationship to a girl's own psyche. This relationship can be expressive of a wide spectrum of possibilities but, because woman's awareness emerges from her body, her initial physical relationship to a father figure is fundamental in her later development as woman, wife and bearer of Mystery

An unconscious incestuous bond between father and daughter involves a primary inter-relatedness between the two which conditions both body and soul, for the one affects the other. Such a relationship has precedence, psychologically, but this, too, can be manifested in many ways. A father may secure the surrender of his daughter's soul by overpowering her physically, becoming molester, batterer, rapist, paedophile, or he may usurp her body and control it by the force of his spiritual principles, precepts and rules, backed by the strength of his patriarchal position (as did the fathers of Nicole and Emily). Further, he may condemn her to a substitute and dark god by abandonment – exclusion, coldness, abstinence from involvement, in short, by forgoing the natural role of father. The axis of this relatedness, father to daughter and vice versa, is determinative in the fullness of her later image of man and her response to him.

The daughter who is endangered is the one who must

rely on a relationship which takes no notice of the body-spirit continuum, for it circumvents conscious encounter with soul Here the father, or any other person who stands in his place, arrogates to himself the role and place of an ultimate god. But, unlike Zeus, he does not surrender his child knowingly to Hades when the time comes, instead, he sacrifices her for his own psychological aims.

There are dangers implicit either way, by withholding her from initiation or letting her go, unyielding to her cries. But the first is equivalent to keeping a girl psychological hostage and denies her most basic right, the freedom to love and to freely dispose of her body in loving. The father who withdraws from conscious relatedness to his daughter withholds from her his side of the tally; for a symbol cannot consciously exist until one takes responsibility for it, which is the same as to consciously relate to it

My survey of the Korē/Persephone myth has been abbreviated and certain parts have thus far been omitted, most notably, the place of Eubouleus, Persephone's offspring, fruit of Hades' plunder, the child born in the Underworld. Korē; returned as Persephone, a woman grown and with a child, a man child, symbolic of her union and potential for fulfilment of a male image. Referring to this transformation, Kerényi writes. 'Since then the world has been what it is for us mortals: full of plant food and full of hope – of hope because the way she first travelled has led to her ever since '[2] Such a statement contains the insight that our lives are a recall, an anamnesis, of the myth, or as Eliade claims. 'It seems that a myth itself, as well as the symbols it brings into play, never quite disappears from the present world of the psyche, it only changes its aspect and disguises its operations.'[3]

More specifically, according to the Homeric Hymn, it was by the counsel of Zeus that Korē was originally released to the embrace of Hades and, also, according to his counsel that the earth opened to receive them It was also the consequence of divine counsel (*boule*) that events came to pass as they did and the name of the child, Eubouleus, is related to the *boule* (divine counsel, decision, wisdom, will, reflection) by which Korē was originally led to the Underworld to become Persephone, thereby opening the path that others have followed ever since. Likewise, the child that is brought back from her journey into darkness is connected with that selfsame counsel which decreed that she take and complete the journey He is representative of a newborn image of man but nevertheless, is also an inheritance of her father, marked by his features.

Mythic references, like poems and fairy tales, resonate from a self-enclosed world once removed from our own, a world where people live archetypally, unsullied by the exigencies of human existence. But Emily's world was a troubled one for many years, reminding us that the korē introduces us to a myth of resurrection and transformation; yet, when the natural rhythmic unfolding of the archetypal pattern is interfered with, what a woman has to undergo is not sacrifice but ordeal. The inclination of an initiation reflective of the *boule* of Zeus, is toward life enhancement but this depends, too, upon how a woman faces the rite, what she brings to it, her individual temperament, yet also how she has been prepared, the summation and heritage of all that she has met of masculine (and feminine) in her former life. Her initiation can be expressed as a juxtaposition of natures, her own as woman and the changing image of her once and future father

'Once upon a time' the path to the Underworld was opened and Persephone took this path into the darkness as booty and bride of the subterranean god with whom she consummated her marriage as marriages are consummated here on earth and to whom she bore a child as women bear children here above. The result was productive and hopeful and by re-enactment it sustained generations of initiates at Eleusis. But, could it have influenced people in the same way, excepting for the vision they were prepared to receive, an image of Korē/Persephone, authenticated at the climax of their initiations? Her myth conformed to their psychological readiness and, so, gave that vision particular credibility. Had not personal experience and image confirmed one another, wouldn't initiates have turned aside and looked to other myths as more expressive of their conditions?

When I began to investigate the question of how it happened that Jen, Lisa and others had come as they did and so late to initiation, I had to ask whether they were not women whose lives had somehow been diverted from a natural mythic course. At least, their psychological development had been interfered with and, if I were to find the mythic counterpart of their conditions, I would have to look to other mythologems than those set forth in the story of Korē/Persephone. For Jen, Lisa and others like them, there were no conscious and counselled transformations during adolescence, no regeneration. Eubouleus was not a comprehensible figure for them; he could not be conceived, had not been born in their psyches

The women who are the subject of this book did not provide the most extreme examples of psychological interference, they were not the most disturbed women with whom I have worked. But, nevertheless, their lives revealed certain inhibiting continuities, foremost among them being a sustained dependence upon the judgement of their personal fathers. None of these fathers were particularly distinctive men, either, in terms of worldly accomplishment and yet, whether they were conscious of it or not, their influences had been basic and basically determinative in accenting later difficulties in their daughters' lives.

Noticeably, none of the women described herself as pleased with her own life or as yet fulfilled. Consequently, each of them lacked both a sense of belonging and adequacy. They did not necessarily blame men for this (though sometimes they did), or their parents, either mothers or fathers. Mostly, they blamed themselves, speaking self-critically as if they had failed to complete unwanted and difficult tasks that someone else had set for them, with which they had been 'landed' inexplicably and without warning and as to the meaning of which they were still in the dark. They came into analysis lacking precisely what initiates at Eleusis must have received, a vision of renewal involving faith, practice, myth and image inter-related and confirmed by personal experience. Unwittingly, they sought from me the 'counsel' that would respect their needs and relate to them appropriately when it was time for their arrested initiations to be resumed.

Had I met the fathers of these women, or, in at least two instances, the mothers who had assumed father roles even in the presence of yet-living fathers, I might have altered my conclusion. But what the father was really like was less important than the picture of man and father that he bequeathed to his daughter and that she used as a working model in transactions with her own self-image, other men and her God. None of the five was a virgin and, yet, somewhere, they were unawakened. Whatever their sexual experiences had been, in their souls they had not yet undergone transformation 'nor yet known a man'.

Even though the life circumstances of these women varied so markedly and they were of such differing temperaments, more and more I began to notice similarities in their psychological responses toward others, toward themselves and toward me. They resisted genuine human contact. They were aloof, somehow remote and emotionally inaccessible. However dependent, they took pride in their self-sufficiency, their ability to survive, to cope; they made relatively few conscious demands It was characteristic of them that the most important events in their lives occurred when they were alone, in solitude and seclusion They were not persons with whom others easily shared their needs. Their self-esteem, though markedly weak, was inflatedly out-of-proportion internally, personified by animus figures who were elevated, impassive, driving, strong-willed and relentless. At the same time, they were unmoved by symbolism, difficult to penetrate intellectually, emotionally or otherwise.

Less and less did these women suggest the korē wisely counselled and become Persephone. As time went on, my thoughts were more often attracted to the fate of another mythic child, Iphigenia, daughter of Agamemnon. In the Iliad her father is described as a proud and passionate man but vacillating of purpose and easily discouraged. He was indecisive and ambivalent in command, with a slackness reflected in the failure of favourable winds to rise and sweep his battle-ready troops to combat in Troy. But he adored his daughter

The goddess Artemis, provoked by Agamemnon's angry invasion of her sacred precinct and the killing of her sacred deer to feed his men, demanded in return for the gift of rising winds the sacrifice of Iphigenia. Here, again, Agamemnon vacillated but finally acquiesced. Thus it was that the fierce and distant virgin goddess of parturition and guardian of all stillborn children, was able to claim the youthful Iphigenia as priestess and korē forever.

There were striking parallels between certain character traits ascribed to Agamemnon and those referred to as belonging to the fathers of the five women who consulted me. When each described her own make-up, at first I found the profiles corresponded most vividly to those of persons with narcissistic character disorders.[4] But what helped even more was to think of them as 'narcissistically wounded persons', a term employed by another analyst and colleague, Dr Kathrin Asper [5] The women *were* narcissistically wounded, taking the term as descriptive of someone wounded by narcissism. They had each of them been wounded by the narcissism of their fathers, this was the character of the initial experience which had most significantly influenced and arrested their feminine development.

Agamemnon beguiled Iphigenia to the sacrificial altar of Artemis by a ruse He promised her the handsome, fine Achilles as husband. Later, when she learned the truth about his decision, although tormented, she conformed to her father's need. What ensued was not her initiation into womanhood but an heroic withstanding of an ordeal. Convinced that there was no other way, she submitted to the rule laid down by father command and, essentially, all that remained for her thereafter was a life possessed by spirit. Refusing to face his own initiatory task, Agamemnon projected it on to his daughter. Identified both with Agamemnon, her father, and with Hellas, her fatherland, she committed her body to the flames.

To be sacrificed to Artemis was to be surrendered to the protectress of the weak and immature in the sense of ungrown. Living sacrifices to this goddess were not unknown In Hermione and Ageira, Artemis herself was called Iphigenia, for both women were unripened, of astounding beauty, remote, solitary, playful, fond of distance, beloved only of a brother. Artemis was attendant to women at times of irremediable pain, present in travail, honoured by midwives, nurses and nurslings. She mirrors the divine femininity of nature, unmatched, unwed to counsel, unsoftened by maternity. Her anger begets death.[6]

When reading the story of Iphigenia, whether it has been retold by persons of such different faith and temperament as Euripides and Goethe, one is made aware of references which suggest a woman's archetypal identification with untamed and unstructured girlhood To be untamed and unstructured renders her particularly vulnerable, physically and spiritually. By comparison with Persephone, Iphigenia is neither initiated nor transformed. Instead, her body is delivered as ransom for her father's wilful neglect of his soul's own task; as a consequence, her spirit is raped for his purposes. The broken promise is *not* a 'breakthrough of life' into the 'world of Logos security' and does not result in 'a breakthrough to another level of consciousness'.[7]

After her sacrifice, Agamemnon believed his daughter to be dead, as did her mother, whose anger took the form of revenge years later when she murdered her husband. But Artemis had removed Iphigenia from the sacrificial flames, putting in her place a young doe, a substitution which symbolises the offering up to the goddess' divine will of the naive animal or physical side of the girl's nature Once that was consumed, her life became a matter of obedience to unchanging and alien order, the performance of ceremonies that did not transform and stillborn hope.

The goddess bore the child away to a far island of consciousness where she successfully resisted the repeated seductions of a king, and systematically repelled all male intruders – until the appearance, long afterward, of her lost brother, Orestes. He made his escape with her eventually and was able to return her to her fatherland of Greece. But there, again, she remained inaccessible, a priestess as she had been in exile, alone in the temple of Artemis, her goddess-protector. The wound inflicted by way of the self-referring father of her girlhood denied her the epiphany of renewal available to Persephone and offered to later initiates at Eleusis.

Looked at from a woman's perspective, this is a myth of arrested initiation and growth. Rupture of the primary relationship occurs and there is a soul-marking quality inherent in the girl's experience of betrayal, the rending of trust, her salvation by Artemis and her subsequent adaptation. But the will to power is substituted for the counsel of reflection when her father seduces her to the altar There is no discovery of individual significance in the experience and her understanding of such a fate goes no further than conformity and obedience to unchanging and immutable precept Anger is either repressed or projected upon male figures ever after. She remains in the Underworld. There is no resurrection and no meaning unfolds in her life on earth

The split between the masculine and feminine sides of Iphigenia's nature, spirit and body, does not heal By counsel of Artemis rather than Zeus, she is diverted from destruction and placed on a threatened and inaccessible island of consciousnes from which men are systematically excluded by command of the ruling animus-king. There she resides cut off, never reborn, ever subject to her patron goddess of parturition as image of the feminine, eternally liminal, unable to unite the two sides of a woman's being Her love, excepting for an infantile attachment to her brother Orestes, lacks warmth and evidence of trust. Without the capacity to imagine change, she becomes the victim of unchanging images. She endures and survives her resentful seclusion but does not ripen into maturity

Lest we too hastily draw conclusions only from myth, however, we must take into account the psychological inheritance of the individual woman It is slow, painstaking work, the work of analysis, where we consciously compile a psycho-biography that is feelingly recalled in fantasy. But, if such an anamnesis or recall differs from the retelling of a myth because it is personal, it differs also from a case history in that it is subjective and individual. As the story emerges, a woman reveals and discovers herself in the telling and is able to name herself by her own name, rather than that of a patient or someone possessed by an archetypal force, i.e the animus. Perhaps like Jen, or Amanda, she may eventually be enabled to recognise herself as she, myself, a human being and worthy of respect

When, however, we imagine her – Jen, Lisa, Emily or anyone else, wandering in her soul like Korē or waiting, a psychic outcast, like Iphigenia, separated from the one who holds the other side of her *symbolon*, the matching side of a broken tally, we face the realisation that the way back to a lost or missing father who symbolises the restoration of movement and meaning in life will necessitate a profound compensatory relationship. This relationship must be with someone upon whom can be projected the Hades element as well as that of Zeus, the one who as the dark, unseen and unknown other side of father fulfilled the supreme god's intent, resulting in the transformation of a daughter human and divine.

Such a relationship called for by a counsel superior to

our own and met with in analysis is called transference.[8] The term 'transference' refers to a natural psychological tendency to project and 'transfer' the dependency of psychic growth onto someone else at a time of crisis and change. What is transferred is, in its most basic definition, the inability to transform as needed. And the projection, for so it is, is of two kinds, one material and the other spiritual. The analyst is expected to have the resources necessary to *cause* change and to *withstand* it But are not the same expectations made of doctors and of priests and directed to parents and marriage partners, especially to the natural and original father/parent?

Even though a girl may direct an unconscious appeal to her doctor, her analyst or priest to mediate her initiation, like Zeus, when the time comes to do so, he eschews involvement as a person. He plays his part by allowing her space to integrate what she perceives is happening by virtue of her own reflection but this does not render him cold or unloving. It is only that his love takes a different form from that which is personal; it is directed instead to love of soul and his attention is concentrated on the resolution of that which has destroyed the balance of psyche/soul. The doctor relates by way of the physical body; the priest by way of spirit; and the psychologist by way of a psychic dilemma. Where the split is manifest, he takes his place but he approaches it, insofar as he can, without prejudice on the side of either body or spirit. His focus is upon the symbol which unites both

As we have said, the process of initiation moves by way of the metaphorical, dictated neither by precept nor pathology alone but by an inner necessity to transform and signify in the process of becoming It springs from a creative and archetypal impulse to found a new order of being and the labour of analysis itself is dedicated to the translation of conscious story into its dark and pathological components with the subsequent investigation of possibilities from an unconscious and mythic point of view. In the shadow of the archetype are concealed the seeds of its healing and the complement of the endangered daughter's living story is inherent in the symbolism of the unconscious. But she cannot connect with it since she has never made contact with her own mystery and, therefore, symbolism holds neither hope nor value for her as yet. So, if at all, it is in the crucible of a transference relationship that the clinical and the symbolic combine with the possibility of metaphorical re-initiation or the telling onward of an interrupted story. Here metaphor signifies psyche's attempt to become other or heal itself.

Rarely in analysis will two people become lovers and wed. But, almost always, we are asked to love in service of transformation either of the body-image or the spirit-image. Neither is our province; but there are temptations both ways and, so, we easily lose our way. Or, like Agamemnon, the father of Jen and countless others, we opt out and the heritage to woman is endangering to her capacity to bridge the psychic schism ever again. The rupture of trust does not heal and her own attempts overcompensate on the side of the spirit, for she must find a god who will countenance what has taken place in order for her to endure the injustice of something which cannot be otherwise explained. 'When the tension between the incest desire and prohibition is obliterated, fragmentation results and the essential internal union between feminine/masculine opposites is not possible '9

Work with woman is particularly hazardous because of the role that physicality plays in her life as harbinger of change and guardian at the threshold of spiritual perception It may help to be reminded of Hermes here, the one who could travel between upper and lower worlds, the messenger whom Zeus sent to bring back Korē/Persephone. That role is psychologically ascribed to the symbol and to Hermes is transferred the role of symbol-carrier

Like Hermes, we are also symbol-carriers and either the body or the spirit side of our natures can be employed for this purpose. But, to inflate that function in ourselves is

again hybris. When Hermes himself was initiated, insofar
as a god can ever be initiated, Zeus took care to deprive
him of his magic wand, subjecting him eternally to his
own *ultimate* command. Like Hermes, who was only par-
tially divine, we do not reside in a spirit world or in the
world of the flesh entirely. We, too, have access to the
underworld of the unconscious, the realm of madness and
death. We also carry messages between three realms and
ourselves become living symbols Yet, to relate healingly
to another, we must relate psychologically. This is a challenge; to love the soul and the unique personhood of the
other as herself.

Our primary task is concerned with initiation, rather
than with counselling, conversion or wedding. Consciously we know that but to perform the task requires us also to
love, not to seem to love, and it is this which sweeps us
into unknowing and indecision. Indecision is made even
more devilish if we think we know the precept, personal
or professional, in obedience to which we are acting. In
every transformative encounter between two people there
comes a moment when each must recognise, '. . . and I
love'. Then follows the question, 'But, loving, what must I
do?'

The transference exists so that we re-enact unconsciously something which later we are able to integrate consciously. This does not excuse our blundering but imposes
a discipline to submit our reactions and what we do, like
Hermes, to an ultimate possibility which includes but is
greater than either instinct or law, license or boundary,
the actual or the symbolic (i e the clinical or the metaphorical) This is, as it was at Eleusis, visualised as a mystery
before which we become humbled and earthed, yet by
way of which suffering is validated. In the mutual acknowledgment of that mystery is the resolution of the
transference and the realisation of an authentic and authenticated attitude toward that which is sacred, surprising
and supraordinate to what is purely personal

If transference does not go beyond consciousness of

what we already are able to 'see', it falls short of its purpose. We then re-enact the rescue of Iphigenia in the flesh, suggested by the passage with Orestes, but that is all. The tests of loving experienced in analysis, no less so than in life, are involving, as they were for Zeus, of demands made by body and spirit intertwined. But something else than either takes precedence. This, ultimately, is a commitment to the unrealised soul.

When I look back at how initiation took hold of my five analysands and myself, though I might have been persuaded otherwise at certain moments, I now discern that the challenge was always in obedience to an end other than the 'so that' which I thought I foresaw and which provided a plausible answer to our difficulties at the time. For example, I am aware that my deep, treacherous respect and love for Amanda, a love which sustained us through frustrating and tormented periods, was not *so that* she would either become a mother or realise her desire for an inner, as opposed to an outer child. In my view, the latter would merely have spiritualised her initial dilemma. Our confirmed feeling now is that it was *so that* she would be able to freely dispose of her loving body in response to the demands of her individual psyche or soul.

All human activity has a symbolic character, i.e. it points beyond itself to a further reality Since the time of Freud and Jung, psychologists have become skilled at reading symbolic meanings from everyday life This sometimes leads to interpretation on the basis of 'tit for tat' or making what can be called 'psychic translations'. When this happens, analytic work limits itself to consciousness of what is known and it categorises the gods or God To stay with mystery, we'll have to stay with the dilemma or split, remain in liminality and suffer initiation along with those with whom we work. 'But loving, what must we do?'

Not everyone is strong enough or patient enough, or wise enough to stay with unknowing, 'looking into the abyss of the seed', until an answer other than the one that has been expected reveals itself. Nor are we always humble enough to acknowledge that our meaning is more than what we can consciously discern. Perhaps strength and humility begin with our saying, 'I *don't* know'. But one unwilling or unable to allow Hermes to be re-enacted replays the archetypal Agamemnon/Iphigenia sequence and the original wound is reinforced. Body may be rescued but within resides a damaged soul wherein is hidden the personhood of the other.

What counsel commands the release of a daughter to a fate not decreed or desired by a father or father-substitute, mythic or personal? Is it power alone that perpetuates an untimely and unhealthy incestuous bond? Whatever impels us willingly to exercise incest responsibility and forgo usurping a girl's body along with her spirit? Here, ultimately, we face our own god-images, knowingly and unknowingly, wittingly and unwittingly Aware or not, we meet the deity to whom we are willing to make sacrifice, surrendering the already valued to something which is more highly valued. In the case of an analyst, is professionality itself enough to establish and maintain a searching commitment to soul or psyche?

In myth, as we have seen, the same divine powers appear in different personifications and do so simultaneously. Thus, Persephone is at one and the same time Queen of the Underworld, her father's daughter, a mother's child These conditions co-exist in an individual as well and from them a unique person emerges. Unlike Iphigenia, she does not remain possessively obsessed with archetypal dependence. The difference is in the integrity of being fully who one is, a singular likeness in response to an eternal image of infinite magnitude. We who sacrifice and forgo incestuous relationships with those whom we love remain loyal and steadfast to this principle which I have called the 'personhood' of the other It is to assure this that rites are devised. They follow the design of that which is emerging in likeness and by individual response to an inexhaustible image.

It would appear that both clinical practice and professional writing on the subject have presented the alternatives of masculine/feminine involvement during analysis as those of 'acting out' or 'symbolisation'. 'Spiritualisation' might be a better word to describe the latter. What has received less attention is the fact that these are the opposites which exist, are unconsciously combined and manifest their union in initial transference phenomena, dreams and projections of many kinds.[10] The later coniunctio, however, spoken of as 'the goal', is a conjunction of opposites in obedience to a third, transcendent principle which takes precedence over either of the previous two It is for this that the child, the *lapis*, the alchemical gold or *verdigris* stand It is for the achievement of this, a psychic phenomenon with personhood as its obvious expression, that the incest impulse and the incest taboo are essential.

Speaking with understanding about symbolic relationship, Sherrard writes.

It is only when it is perceived that there is an inherent, if concealed, correspondence or con-generacy between the reality which the symbolism is intended to signify and the matter to which it is applied, that the symbolism is able to operate as a transmuting or transforming agency.[11]

This encompasses the consciousness expected of an analyst. It conditions his attitude and should make it possible for him (or her) to undergo the difficult transformative process alongside and alongwith his analysand (initiate). Yet, he himself, the analyst, in recognition of the magnitude and the intent of the image, works consciously on the threshold or at the border between the 'I was' and the 'I am-not-yet' of the one for whom he is companion.

Still, the analyst alone among psychotherapists is committed to the healing of the body/spirit split rather than to compensation in one direction or the other. Here the symbol functions as an overarching bridge, a soul suture which is embedded in flesh on both sides Inevitably, at some stage, attention will need to be given to the wisdom but not to definition of the divine arch-image which acts as surgeon of the soul.[12] Definition is the function of a theologian or priest. For an analyst to say at a time of tension or crisis, 'It is only symbolic', unconsciously pre-empts and also usurps that place for he assigns the matter to the realm of spirit; the other extreme being to surrender it to body and its impulses. But a symbol rightly under-stood mysteriously partakes of both.

The resolution of transference will be a testing of trans-ference, a testing that must withstand a felt betrayal as it did for Korē; and, here, again, the one who betrays is identified as father. Psychologically perceived, behind the mother who betrays is always the principle which causes her to do so, a *logos* both honoured and feared by woman. And it will be predictable, psychologically, that '(the woman) who has no father is forced to become her own'.[13] But when betrayed and before making her response, she lingers for a while in liminality, bereft of an author, au-thority and authenticity for her life. If, later, as she recov-ers a sense of authorship in her life, she still suspects that her partner did not fully participate in the liminal experi-ence but 'knew it all the time', that he did not suffer as she suffered nor with the same wound, she feels that he man-ipulated her and she becomes vengeful. Identifying with Iphigenia, a woman then sees herself as many women (not all of them feminists) now do, as having been laid upon the altar, a blood offering to man and a father's prior designs

To test the experience of betrayal inherent in transfer-ence and to recover its meaning, there must be acceptance of an erotic element in psyche that transcends use of the body as there is a teleological purpose that overrides or overarches mere reason. As in marriage there is a supra-natural union of two people, by way of transference there is a supranatural union of psychic elements. In a rela-tionship where father and daughter images are constel-lated, father represents the active, creative and purposeful principle of the individual. The gift of he who makes it impossible to live through and by way of a woman's initial transference not only betrays her trust in this image but reinforces a fear of creativity in any form. The aim of symbolic or transference encounter is to assure that what is outer and literal be taken in and used metaphorically; i e. creatively and psychologically, which is to say, individually

The participation of initiator and initiate in a sanctified loving relationship which allows for mutual exploration and exchange seems to have a soul-impressing quality and determines the outcome. Therefore, we cannot speak about initiation apart from transference or vice versa since the only group into which a person can be initiated is a group whose souls have been similarly touched and tried. At that time, the time of initiation, body, spirit and soul interact. To neglect any one of the three is to lose touch with the coherence of the whole.

As for myself, I wish to make it clear that Lisa, Emily and the others did not teach me 'about' the transference. Rather, they taught me certain things or led to my discovering insights 'by way of' the transference A few of my insights have been shared in this book, others have been personal, but all of them have led to further meanings.

Certainly it was Jen who first made me aware of the recurring importance of initiation in a woman's life and who demonstrated how creatively pent-up psychological energy withheld by father-subjection can express itself once it is allowed release. Nicole's rite bore fruit in my investigation of the eros/logos, body/spirit split. Lisa's experience drew my attention to the place of the sacred and the meaning of sacrifice in a fully developed relationship. Emily confronted me as no one else had with the limitations of my profession in the presence of live transference. Amanda, however, initiated me into vivid consciousness that the initiatory process involves a transmutation of image and likeness together; it is a progression, not an event.

A woman goes on for as long as she is able to depend upon the adequacy of an image she has 'seen' and transmuted into likeness. But, when she is unable to do so any longer, she submits herself, however painfully, to the challenge of initiation for the sake of her renewed image and changed likeness. So long as she does not encounter another to whom she can ascribe absolute importance and grant primacy of status, however, one in whom she can have trust and who will awaken her to a consciousness of her essential nature (which is not the same as a correction of her arrested nature), the energy for transformation is never released.

She may discover her partner subjectively or in real terms; but, in either case, the companion needs to be a figure whom a woman is able to love devotedly and with all her mind, soul and body. The one she encounters in reality or in fantasy must be equally as vulnerable and as committed as herself but with the difference that he remains an 'other', complementing her with a corresponding but not identical response. Then he is capable of assuming a symbolic resemblance to the psychic carrier of what she needs but has not yet found psychologically 'Only in the union of two creatures of the same nature and of equal significance, yet in every respect distinct as to form is the creation of the new man – the whole man – possible.'[14] . . And it has the effect of restoring the divine image to man, since in such a union one encounters the paradoxical presence of an intervention personally relevant but, seemingly, transcendently intentioned.

In a loving relationship which can overcome ego defences sufficiently to engender trust, a woman transfers to an 'other' her ability to transform. Upon this partner she projects what her original lover was not. Inevitably this new lover to whom she is now attracted symbolises what was missing before. In the course of her relations with such a figure a way can be found back to the missing father and, consequently, a path ahead to renewal is at the same time disclosed. An otherwise baleful sequence is thereby dignified and enriched by fulfilment of a compensatory rather than solely a corrective possibility involving the difficult maturation of a psychologically static woman. When this happens, whether within or without analysis, a girl is grown. Her first initiation is completed, and others can follow, each bringing her closer to a likeness of her individual self.

The *visio beatifica* which was granted to initiates at Eleusis was not an outcome of the mysteries but an image of their essence, for the shared relationship between man and woman not only reproduces life in time but also recreates it for eternity. It is an inflation to think we can ever consciously embody the complete Mystery; yet, we can be aware that our lives also carry and convey mystery. With consciousness of this differentiation we approach humility and also incorporate a religious attitude. Turner concludes: 'The powers that shape the neophytes in liminality for the incumbency of a new status are felt, in rites all over the world, to be more than human powers, though they are invoked and channeled by the representatives of the community.'[15]

Unless we, analyst-companions, are prepared for the unexpected encounter with mystery, its summons, once delivered to the soul, may be diverted, wasted or abused. In this instance, the choice is ours. But, if this happens, the sacred nature of the summons, denied and unacknowledged, converts itself into destructive shadow once it is repressed.

On the other hand, if acknowledged and accepted as sufferable but not-yet-to-be-known, the summons assists the healing of an endangered woman by rescuing her from what amounts to a threat of psychic death. Like Iphigenia, she would fill out her days with endless repetitions of meaningless ceremonies while at the same time unconsciously longing to be reunited with the father of whom she was deprived. If life moves on and develops for her, change is enabled by a symbolism uniquely individual while at the same time capable of combining what was formerly sundered in the soul; nascent woman and person with an inadequate image and appreciation of man as well as a limited vision of his significance for she, herself.

CHAPTER 6

. . . AND EVER VIRGIN*

All that she became was nascent in the image but was not itself
the image
Lossky, 'Panagia'

Between the image of Korē and that of Mary the Virgin lie not only a few hundred years of human history but also the Incarnation. That is to say, the two images are connected but they are not the same. One is the prototype of the feminine initiate but the other is God-bearer. The story of the first, a child of gods, conveys to humans that their earthly bodies are carriers of mystery and meaning. The second, human, naturally accepts this as an attribute of her earthly destiny. 'Ripe for marriage' they both were, but virgins with a difference.

Historical attempts to establish the place of Mary the Virgin to some extent reflect the image of what she was but, at the same time, obscure it. From a psychological perspective, firstly, she symbolises the opening of body to access and completion by soul. Without full and conscious awareness of the implication of her role, she nevertheless allows

* The term 'ever Virgin' is found in the Conciliar Acts of the Christian Church from the Fifth Council onwards but has not been expounded by the Councils which have used it.

herself to become the matrix for a divinely purposed transformation. Only afterward, it is written, does she reflect
upon the import of the annunciation which was given to
her, pondering these things in her heart. With impregnation of the divine Spirit and by relating to that lovingly
and as a sacred responsibility, she brings to birth a child
spoken of as Saviour, human and divine.

The world's most widely acknowledged festival com-
memorates the miraculous birth of her child, celebrated
everywhere as coincident and synonymous with the return of light And so, to a woman she personifies her own
soul, the place where the Logos or archetype of the Divine
Patriarch confronts and embraces her humanity, needing
body to be embodied. To a man the Virgin gives the
incarnation of his ultimate meaning. To persons of both
sexes she projects the image of the promise of redemption.
The life of her son is framed by two envisionings: the first,
the *promise* of light over darkness, and the other the
triumph of resurrection, coincident with the return of fertility to a barren earth

In this instance, as in that of the korē, the telesponse of
a virgin prepared people to 'see' a principle incarnate. But,
as Korē became known as Queen of the Underworld,
Mary the Virgin became Queen of Heaven. Her spontaneous telesponse initiated for her a unique place in history and for the world a new kind of person. No doubt as
divine spouse and Queen of Heaven she is more than
what we perceive in the image of her being and role but it
is these which are the concern of the psychologist. Interpretations of why the event happened to her when and as it
did; i.e. its cause, and suppositions as to its finality must be
left to others, which, of course, is true of all case histories.

Yet, like Korē, Mary the Virgin is also related to an
image of woman transforming. Within her tradition, the
tradition of the Church, this is Eve. She is known as the
second Eve, but whereas Eve became mother of men,
Mary the Virgin became the Mother of God.[1]

Layard cites a sermon of St Bernard's in which he gives

a graphic description of Eve as the diseased will, 'that lady who lies at home paralysed and grievously tormented' and 'who, when commanded by the Reason (Logos) to amend her ways, leaps forth in her fury, forgetful of all her weakness, (exclaiming). "why is not the Reason ashamed of such an attack, such an onslaught upon the wretched will? Is this", she asks, "all your conjugal fidelity? Is this the way you feel for me when I suffer so much?" ' St Bernard ends his sermon with the challenging exhortation to his listeners: 'Thou (who) are bound to the will, strive to relax the bond which thou canst not break The will is thy Eve.'[2]

Layard uses this passage as illustrative of Eve personified as a projection of man's anima. But can we not also see the passage as a reflection of woman poisonously entwined with an all-powerful animus or god-image while at the same time struggling to differentiate and gain mastery over herself? Are not Eve's cries suggestive of liminal woman who refuses to accept the death of her previous incestuous fantasies in relation to an idealised father/lover/god – Korē betrayed, the aggrieved Demeter, Jen? Mary the Virgin, by contrast, takes the necessary death of a previous fantasy upon herself, integrating it in service to a more informed and generous image of the Logos. Herein lies the difference between receipt of what is perceived as an enunciation or dictum and what is accepted as an annunciation or prelude to transformation

According to an apocryphal story reported by James, Mary the Virgin was spinning when the Angel of the Annunciation appeared to her Commemorated again and again in icons of the Eastern Church we see the moment when, in wonder at the apparition of the angel, she drops her spindle and questions whether she is worthy to be so chosen. Then, in the time that it takes only to drop and recover the spindle, she readies herself to respond with an instinct that offers itself to be transformed (and, so, to transform) in accordance with the divine Will. Insofar as the response of the first Eve was a purely human response, and, therefore, linked to body alone, it was ego-orientated while that of the second, Mary the Virgin, is a soul's response, linking body and spirit with a higher purpose and, therefore, self-orientated.

Responsive to the self, she later gives birth to its likeness.[3] In a woman's experience of initiation, this second Eve has a significance greater than any enumeration of her attributes can reveal. Her image is arresting and awesome but Jen would have looked at me with shock and terror had I ever mentioned the Virgin Maria; in the early days Lisa would have quit analysis at the suggestion of any kind of symbolic likeness Like Korē, Mary the Virgin was not to be used a model. But, nevertheless, her likeness became important while working with these women

For only a woman who has virginity can lose it, i.e. be initiated. As I have indicated, not one of the five had consciously possessed it prior to analysis. Their virginity and their perceptions of themselves as virgin had been tampered with Still, I have described the psychological or soul state of these women as that of 'not yet having known a man'. When the completing 'other' of their lives appeared would there also appear in them a likeness to virginity of which they had hitherto been unconscious; and, if so, would they be able to recognise it? This was a question which recurred for me.

Virginal they were (or, perhaps, a more apt word would be arid) if one looks at the image in terms of a spectrum of archetypal possibilities. But did any of them have the capacity to consent to a summons to be herself and respond to it fully, as if called by her God, combining in herself, as Mary the Virgin combined, divine function and human person? And, could she then carry what would be conceived full-term without abortion or miscarriage even though the wisdom of its design remained a mystery? This I had come to associate with the one who holds a place unique among women, who combines in herself readiness of body and virginity of spirit.[4]

None of the women was destined for a vocation in

religious terms and I didn't expect miracles. Yet, I was quite sure that if any of them could recall the spontaneous capacity to say 'yes' to what she asked for herself, this would be equivalent to willing herself to be the one of whom she was capable. And the effect would seem miraculous because it would conform to the fullness of her unrealised natural capacity and it would be transformative of her person and her future

Then came the day when without warning Amanda announced that she was not going to conceive a child. She was going to write a book and the announcement struck me as a reversal, a denial of herself and our efforts. At that moment I could not help but 'see' her decision as indicative of a kind of regression. Our labours together had been in terms of a growing awareness of her physical body, toward integration of the many previous dreams of Aunt Marina who had watched over her child on the floor below while she, Amanda, worked at her desk on a balcony above, and in preparation for a late but, as she professed, a much desired pregnancy

The announcement seemed to bring us to a cul-de-sac rather than point to the beginning of a path on the way to psychic renewal and insight. I was shocked. We had been sitting face to face with one another and I had been looking down. I looked up and shook my head as if to shake off my bewilderment and disbelief. I frowned.

As it transpired, the announcement was an end but it was also a beginning, though a beginning inexpressible in terms immediately available to the consciousness of either of us. Later, in the disclosure of the way which opened out from this decision and the immediate rupture of our initially trusting relationship, we both saw Amanda revealed as herself, or, more accurately, we underwent a series of experiences together that taught us both (if 'taught' is the appropriate word) that true virginity is not a hypostasis but the power to hypostasise in a given situation.[5] This took time. But what I mistook in that moment as symbolic of wound was actually indicative of its healing Mary the Virgin had the capacity to discern the difference immediately.

Perhaps other therapists would explain what took place in terms of other imageries but to Amanda and me it became important that we were involved with the imagery of the virgin Among other ways in which it was relevant, the worship of Mary the Virgin pertained directly to the subject matter of her chosen labour. The fact that neither of us at times was *any* daughter struggling with any mother but that together we were met by *this* mother and confronted by *that* father challenged our individuality in a hazardous, uniquely significant and personal way

When the crunch came – and it was heralded by her announcement – my initial response bypassed my best intentions and what I perceive to have been her psyche's need. The frown did not escape her notice and with that gesture I became another in the line of mother/father/ lovers who appropriated her brilliance and artistry for their own purposes and status, ignoring her own deepest desires. A look of fear passed over her face and she blurted out defiantly but impressively, 'Actually, it isn't going to be all that easy, you know. I'm scared stiff!' With only that much forewarning, it seemed as if virginity recognisably manifested itself on her behalf and confronted me 'So what are you going to do about it?' she challenged. 'It will be *my* project, you realise. *I've* chosen it. *I'll* do it.'

The time of the dropping of the spindle for me, symbolically, came with the summons of the bell which signalled the arrival of my next analysand. I left the room to answer it. Although I would do myself and the profession a disservice if I did not acknowledge that there had been months, perhaps years of careful preparation for that moment, between the time when I left Amanda and returned I took a deep breath. Face to face with her once again, I replied, 'Yes, it *is* yours – and I am with you; I'll be there.'

When she had gone and working hours were over for the night, I had cause to regret and time to ponder. Amanda had not come to me asking for instruction about how to live her life. She was 'growing a woman' and today she had somehow claimed her status and authority, perhaps for the first time as herself and in response to a unique and personal summons The time had come for me to love her in a new way. Her pregnant abilities were sacred and it must become sacred to me that she freely dispose of them.

The fact that the book was on a sacred subject did not ensure that writing it was part of a life's vocation but it might be Analysis was not Amanda's church and I was not her spiritual guide We would consider these things together and in our hearts, so as to speak. But was I not ready to trust that in the exploration she could become aware of the psychic dimensions of a church and re-imagine the image of guide within herself? And must I not be willing to submit to transformation of my own images alongside her?[76]

To better comprehend the virginity of Mary the Virgin, we have to envision her as standing on a boundary between created and uncreated worlds with the ability to say 'yes' to that which is creating. For centuries painters of many faiths have tried to capture that moment of her assent. Often what they have painted has revealed more of them or their times than of her but she is expressed as humble, ready, obedient, willing. This is the 'unchrist-ened image' 'It consists of everything that is sequent to the origin but falls short of the consummation', writes St Maximos the Confessor.[7] All that happens later flows from this Standing there and at that moment, ripe for marriage, she embodies the essence of the intermediary state She is liminal woman, face to face with her destiny.

The consummation which follows bears only a partial resemblance to her prior state, for otherwise it would not be a fulfillment. Yet, it is not simply the opposite of her previous condition, either; it is instead its fruition. The moment of assent when virginity of spirit is visibly expressed is the moment when choices are acknowledged, though still not assimilated. Assimilation and integration come later; pondering and reflection being apparent in the outcome, reflecting both the child-bearer and her child.

The knowledge that informs one in the time of liminality is not yet gnosis but prepares for gnosis Later one knows that he has seen and what he has seen. Like the initiates at Eleusis, he also knows the inutterable nature of what he has seen, for it has not been thought but impressed upon his being. The liminal condition provides for this progression from beginner to learner to knower of that which one did not previously apprehend ontologically. Within it, the virginal instinct to lend oneself to the creation of soul signifies a moment of balance and the beginning of psychic repose.

Turner speaks of the wisdom that is implanted in ritual liminality as *mana* for it represents the generic authority of the tradition invested in a given community.[8] Here, once more, if we erase the linear or historical distinctions between pagan and Christian, we may better comprehend what happens psychologically. The community, whether tribal or Church, is the repository of the cultures' knowing – its story, its values, dogmas, customs, observances, sentiments and relationships; in short, its laws, its practices, and its myth. 'In liminality', Turner goes on to say, 'the neophyte must be a *tabula rasa*, a blank slate, on which is inscribed the knowledge and wisdom of the group in those respects that pertain to a new status . . . partly a destruction of the previous status and partly a tempering of their essence '[9] Here he describes in anthropological terms virginity of spirit and defines its function in initiation For, it is during the rites that one meets tradition in both unconscious and conscious guise; as 'the other' in direct confrontation and by reference to the group of which one is a part.

With the response of an initiand, her individuality is expressed and seeds are sown for regeneration of herself but also of the tradition as well. So it is that in the tradition of the Christian Church, the unique response of Mary the Virgin. 'Behold the handmaid of the Lord: be it unto me according to thy word' (St Luke 1.38) becomes the redemption of Eve As one among women, she enriches tradition, being she who knows instinctively what she must hear and, more importantly, how she must keep what she hears.[10]

When she is most at one with herself, Mary the Virgin also becomes most at one with her tradition. At the time of the annunciation, she receives an objective presence that comes *to* her and she reifies a subjective content that arises from *within* her.[11] It is, therefore, a combined religious and psychological event, uniting the individual person with her person-hood. By giving her assent, Mary the Virgin indicates that she is one with and ready to take her place in response to the generic authority of a tradition which links her body and spirit with a transcendent or divine purpose.

Here there is counsel for all of us who work as psychotherapists, for those we meet are by and large people who are unaware of or estranged from traditions, most especially those of a religious nature which embrace two realities, each of which remains insufficient or incompleted without the other Often the one tradition to which such people are willing to acknowledge a sense of belonging is merely the tradition of being human. This is a mega-group, a loose amalgam without consciousness of itself The recovery of the virginal instinct presupposes, however, recovery of a sense of belonging to a group with consciousness of its generic authority. It immediately differentiates between an 'I' and a 'Thou', poses problems of relatedness between the two and suggests awareness of the tradition to which that relatedness is relevant.

'It is only through the psyche that we can establish that God acts upon us', Jung writes, 'But we are unable to distinguish whether these actions emanate from God or the unconscious.'[12] The virginal impulse stimulates one to acknowledge and affirm a distinction. Personal analysis makes conscious that recognition, leaving the person free to then match his incompleted *symbolon* of faith and a sense of belonging with a corresponding tradition. The previous or virginal state is uncontaminated – for what purpose? The psychologist's answer can never be specific. Among early Christians and continuing in certain church traditions to the present day, the Logos is defined as that which makes known the image of the Father. Correspondingly, the *Panagia* or response of Mary is that which makes it live in the world

In the work of Jung, especially in his extensive investigations of anima/animus and his formulations of the self, are extrapolations and interpretations of these basic formulations 'It is the psyche which, by the divine creative power inherent in it, makes the metaphysical assertion, it posits the distinctions between metaphysical entities Not only is it the condition of all metaphysical reality, it *is* that reality,' he wrote.[13]

Such statements firmly place Jung within metaphysical or religious tradition but does that make his point of view a-scientific or unreliably biased? Perhaps it is simply more complete. His discernment of the distinction between religious cognition and cognitive religion and his struggles toward integration of these disharmonies within himself increased his importance as the first psychiatrist to formulate and establish religion as empirical and psychological fact He was an innovator in Western traditions by whom theologians and scientists were, understandably, puzzled but among whom there have been those who have been equally grateful.

The formulations hinge upon the unfolding of womanhood as a natural progression toward that which is psychological or religious This truth was expressed in archaic form by Korē whose mythic journey led initiates to see the connection between physis and spiritus. Both she and Mary the Virgin gave archetypal expression to body as the material of transfiguration and the container for divine transformation. The implication for psychology is that in their imagery it confronts the god-image and the limit of its own therapeutic work. Neither of these two, whether we view them as persons or as images and archetypal metaphors, was committed to being virgin but to being herself, used by her god; one unwillingly and as yet unknowingly, the other knowingly and with the humility to say 'yes' to the creator Both risked discovering in fullness what had previously been perceived inert in her soul. By way of them, the image bodies forth its essence as it has never been and has been waiting to be.[14]

Mary the Virgin, when most completely herself, mirrors to us the substance of psyche/soul most fully conscious of *itself* Historically, devotees who have found it necessary to pre-ordain her for this accomplishment take her spiritual existence literally and she becomes one alone of all her sex [15] Here, though, we are looking at her symbolically, psychologically, iconically The opposite would be to speak of her, in contrast to Iphigenia, as a girl who resolved her mother/father complex, which is a perspective morbidly human and limited. All that she became was, indeed, nascent in the image but was not itself the image. Had it been, individual choice or action would have been impossible.

Both she and Korē expose the self as a dark body waiting for penetration by light so that it can be transformed Penetration initiates a new condition by reconstellating the body-spirit union in terms of its relationship to ultimate or divine purposes. 'Individuation appears, on the one hand, as the synthesis of a new unity which previously consisted of scattered particles, and on the other hand, as the revelation of something that existed before the ego and is in fact its father or creator as well as its totality.'[16] When this happens, one's view of oneself as merely human and self-sufficient has to be sacrificed. To take the risk of assent knowingly will be with consciousness of one's own I/Thou relatedness.

Instead of representing chastity of body alone, we now see Mary the Virgin as a condition of soul. It is in this light that she is herself the most fruitful aspect of the archetypal spectrum of virginity. Her polar opposite, the Black Virgin, is not to be thought of only as lascivious and a whore in the carnal sense; she is sterile of soul. Likewise, virginity is a life-long attribute of psyche, whether belonging to man or woman. And St Augustine states: 'Virginity of the flesh belongs to a few; virginity of the heart must be the concern of all.'[17] As anima for a man, the virginity of which we have been speaking safeguards the individuality of himself by its natural connection with mystery; i.e. his ultimate destiny Again, speaking in psychological terms, in later years she is personified for both sexes as the old white woman, wise with a wisdom derived from virginal encounter.

Reflecting upon the virgin as prior to marriage and without the law suggests a freedom to freely love, though in terms of her soul's command. Here without relatedness of an I to a Thou who is totally other, a woman is fettered by obedience to man-made and historic traditions, social, political, professional and otherwise. At some point, therefore, a girl/woman must recognise the wholly other as different from and transcending the personal partner or sexual opposite Otherwise, someone – father, lover or whoever he may be – is burdened with an impossible and inflated projection. Initiation rites delineate aspects of this image but also fulfil it by making explicit the already existing but unconscious bond with what is intuitively felt to be sacred. Since this is an essential part of maturation, full womanhood becomes 'theirs by rite'.

Considering the virgin as unwed emphasises her uncommitted state. Neither body not spirit have yet been promised to another. She isn't engaged; i.e. consciously related to anyone or anything else which can command her *complete* devotion. Yet, she is capable of obedience to that which she was created to be. Obedience here is not obedience to a principle alone, which would be purely spiritual. Neither is it acquiescence or submission to *physis*, which would permit rape of body. It is obedience to realisation of the divine thought, involving both body and spirit, an obedience succinctly expressed in the words of the son of Mary the Virgin reported in the Gospel according to St Luke: 'My mother and my brethren are they that hear the word of God and do it' (Luke 8 19–21).

Woman has her own mode of being, her own form of

existence, which prepares her to make that distinction and
follow it. The soul-impressing quality of her initiatory
rituals merely brings that capacity to her awareness and
places it at her conscious disposal. But self-awareness and
obedience to one's individual principle are evoked, quick-
ened and engendered by love. And, without devotion to a
supraordinate image which embraces and gives priority to
psyche or soul itself, one easily falls victim to the seductions lying in wait on either side of the spirit/body divide.
When this happens, transfiguration and transformation
do not occur. In psychological terms, there is reinforce-
ment of the pre-existing neurotic pattern.

Jung's assertion of a self embedded in each person is an
anticipation of a belief in the virgin to be awakened and
revealed. But the awakening comes by intervention and
acceptance of divinely intended (self-directed) love. Jung's
reticence to express his empirical findings about the self in
religious terminology led him to formulate a symbolically
oriented explanation of the transference couched in
alchemical terminology. Yet, using the symbology of religion, a self-oriented psychology requires obedience to the
virginal moment when spirit meets body and the demands
of soul outweigh either. To formulate it in this way acknowledges the place of woman as a natural expression of
being and removes the patriarchal injunction to act in response to a command. Again, there is no attempt on the
part of the psychologist to define the god one loves and
believes in but any tendency to make a religion of psychology itself is reversed.

So the analyst can write:

To meet you, I must risk myself as I am. The naked
human is challenged. It would be safer reflecting alone
than confronting you. And even the favourite dictum of
reflective psychology – a psychology which has consciousness rather than love as its main goal – 'Know
thyself', will be insufficient for a creative psychology.
Not 'Know thyself' through reflection, but 'Reveal thyself' which is the same as the commandment to love,

since nowhere are we more revealed than in our
loving.'[18]

Or more tested in our faith.

'Love blinds', the writer continues, 'in order to extin-
guish the wrong and daily vision so that another eye may
be opened that perceives from soul to soul.'[19] But this can
happen only to a person by whom a self-summons can be
imagined and received as being no less real than herself.
Then it, rather than its messenger or intermediary, becomes the beloved. Otherwise, all that will be revealed will be
a mirror image of an all too human fantasy projection with
all its limitations; be it partner, husband, divine consort,
analyst or whatever. Initiation by a priest is of a different
order, however, because there it is assumed, implicitly,
that there is unquestioning love of God and the soul of the
initiate as capable of reflecting God.

To what gods have psychotherapists and analysts
attached themselves so that those who seek their help go
on loving the image of them rather than the images of
their own individual souls? We see this happening repeatedly with those who never leave analysis or who con-
fuse recreating the likeness of the analyst with giving birth
to their souls' own offspring Have we here also neglected
or distorted the symbolism of the virgin as soul or matrix
of transformation? And, in so doing, don't we also reveal
ourselves as confined by a dogma?

The body of the Church is guilty of the same practice at
times, incorporating to itself members unconverted to
their vocations But it seems that the analytic tradition,
that of psychology, is particularly susceptible to incomple-
tion if we accept and emphasise that consciousness is our
aim. The ultimate question is consciousness of what? Scientific consciousness *per se* disallows for particularisation.
It attempts to eliminate Mystery by explanation No spindle falls in surprise or wonder; a search for reasons takes
precedence over pondering in the heart. We substitute
decision on the basis of evidence for obedience in response to love. And this prevents our apprehension and

appreciation of that most essential yet enigmatic quality characteristic of Mary the Virgin, her ever-virginity.

Hers is readiness, pure and undefiled, broken and restored ever again In woman the broken and restored, death and life, are ever-present and co-existent images. Each new stage in life requires that she suffer the pain of pondering purpose anew. At the moment when she assents to becoming the God-bearer, Mary the Virgin shows herself to be most at one with her humanity; she discovers her being in process.

The Panagia or response of Mary the Virgin expresses a ripeness of receptivity, a fullness demanded of her over and over again – later, when she gives birth to her son, further when that son comes of age; then, when he performs the first of the so-called miracles and, eventually, when he dies on the cross. She does not represent commitment to a single-minded and unchanging idea or ideal of womanhood. Neither is her response a sign of growth and maturation; that is to say, it is not arrived at in pursuit of a goal such as 'wholeness'. It is simply an opening of herself to the agonising mystery of renewal, a willingness to be defined and redefined by the necessities of her soul. She is pure in advance of the state of completion and initiation does not transform the Virgin; it reveals her and the revelation is her woman-self.

The significance of love is rooted in the revelation of individuality. The fruition of love and the fulfilment of its inspiration is to effect an exchange between those it joins together, an exchange which reveals and unites their distinctive characters as they adapt, each to the other.[20] Therefore, love is directed toward restoration of an original totality. 'Deprivation rightly understood and truly accepted will open the way to a new access of psychic consciousness, which in the end doubles the personality by giving back all that has been sacrificed, in a form that can no more be lost.'[21]

Love satisfies our yearning to signify, a yearning which is sometimes referred to as 'a nostalgia of being'. Whether it be transference love or the conjugal love of marriage, it is aimed at the recovery and disclosure of one's essential and natural being rather than a perfection or improvement of that. From this perspective, we can acknowledge that through love the lost virgin is restored to man.[22] In Jungian terms, she is the unsullied self.

In the risk of loving lies both hope and danger: the hope of integrity, the danger of genitality. The outcome depends on readiness for obedience to that which 'feels right' but is beyond our immediate comprehension, latent, silent, powerful and powerfully affirming, yet undisclosed There is no law of loving. 'Love is a divine truth, dangerously won, a creative act that overcomes the world and all its conditions, essentially free.'[23] This the virgin senses *in potentia* and consciously offers herself as matrix and carrier of that surprising truth. Hers is a readiness to be impregnated with the love of one's being, a readiness that naturally inheres to the body of woman and is reinforced by its rhythms.

It is woman's design to be she who inspires life and she who becomes its carrier. This conditions her psychology and distinguishes her approach to soul as well as to members of the other sex. But her perception is not confined to that and her consciousness moves beyond that In contrast, a man also carries, but what he carries, he carries consciously from the beginning Neither can do the work of the other; they only appear to be able to do so. He reaches Mystery in the revelation of *what* he carries; she finds Mystery by *being* a carrier. The spirit that motivates and substantiates them is the same.

In his remarks pertaining to the Dogma of the Assumption, Jung made the statement that Mary the Virgin was necessary to God; she gave him a human body.[24] But her image is also necessary to us. She is that which bears the enigma of divine impregnation wherever and whenever it occurs and she is found in man or in woman. Hers was a receiving being; *being* used here as synonymous with soul or the vessel where body and spirit are united. And loving consciously will be to involve oneself with awareness of relationship to the consequences of love for the soul. Love's significance is revealed as individuality

The virgin image symbolises the threshold of Mystery or that which can be realised as of consequence to the soul, one's self or individuality. She is faithful to its meaning before it is available to consciousness At the time of the annunciation Mary the Virgin responded as if there were meaning, though import eluded and overwhelmed her. As a whole, her entire life was co-natural with the acceptance of a counsel greater than her own, evident but not yet disclosed. She could consent to it without the reassurance of 'knowing' and bear the consequence freely, having lent herself to its purpose, having given full and free consent. Her acceptance can be likened to a consciousness of her own sanctity, an inner attitude without which the bodily status of being a woman is meaningless.

To be virgin is ours by nature. It is the uninitiated propensity to say 'yes' to what calls, disrupts and yet belongs to us. A sacred symbolism becomes a creative influence in life only when it is allowed ('seen') as capable of acting upon the body or matter to which it applies in such a way that it helps transform this matter into the reality which the symbolism is intended to signify. Here it is the work of the psychologist to awaken a person to the implication of symbol. The work of the priest clarifies and interprets that implication as sacred within a specific context of belief. The liminal quality of transference love is bearable when it can be accepted as symbolic *and* with implication for the realisation of one's self, the being of one's soul. It brings one, inevitably, to the threshold of virginal choice

Paradoxically, when a woman loses her bodily virginity, she is confronted with the mystery of being ever-virgin spiritually. But, to be ever-virgin signifies remaining ever-human, as well. Only with this reference point is a person able to exercise obedience to that which summons both one's humanity and sacrality, body and spirit, psyche or soul. Mary the Virgin mediates that which partakes of both humanity and divinity. Her virginal attitude already anticipates and makes possible this union. She holds the germinal in anticipation of the real, which will be an embodiment of the Logos or Word. She reveals the significance of love in the disclosure of individuality.

In the virgin, we find the seed of our significance but to reach her modern woman has to break all idols and graven images, to submit as Lisa, Emily and Amanda eventually did, to humiliation before rediscovery of a purpose and implication native to their womanhood We cannot be consciously deprived of what we have never known. The recovery of respect and reverence for Mystery is a legitimate quest in psychological initiation but it is possible only with differentiation of the body itself as human though capable of conveying a meaning greater than that confined to itself alone.

The original and virginal possibility of realising the eternal feminine is still present in earthly woman Her body is a manifold symbol, suggesting in multiple forms her propensity as god-bearer. In her nature are the seeds of both material and spiritual expression. For this reason, only when she is fully herself and woman, can she attain to a transcendent or sacred likeness, not to be confused with a purely archetypal manifestation. By contrast, that which is sacred will be uniquely individual It is as an individual that any woman becomes 'she of all her sex'.

Confronted with this possibility, she stops, she prepares by rite, she waits, consents and ponders That which is virginal works against identifying what goes on in the soul with the subjective ego.[25] We are reminded again of the unchristened image; humility is of its essence. The ever-virginal seed is given intact with one's nature. The dropping of the spindle is the loosing of worldly ties, what one had assumed to be the thread of one's existence, in response to being penetrated by summons of the self or divine command. Consciousness of the summons is a matter for psychological analysis but the response is instinctive.

To perceive virginity in this way is to release it from society's reasoned and patriarchal interpretations and restore it to a feminine likeness. Awareness of one's virginal essence is the fruition and goal of woman's initiation. Out of the darkness of her non-being, that which may be is brought into existence. She symbolises reality not yet realised, a consciousness capable of obedience to a destiny realised from within. In her assent is her completion. In woman, Eve and Mary are constant, recurring, ever-present images. 'When God chose, he chose the way of Mary'; when she chose, she chose Him Her gift is a significance borne by human existence.

NOTES

1 THE NATURE OF THE EVIDENCE

1 C.G Jung, *The Collected Works*, vol. VII, Routledge & Kegan Paul, 1966, para. 437.

2 For psychological definitions of *incest* see Andrew Samuels, Bani Shorter and Fred Plaut, *A Critical Dictionary of Jungian Analysis*, Routledge & Kegan Paul, 1986, also Robert Stein, MD, *Incest and Human Love*, Penguin Books, 1974.

3 Gerardus Van der Leeuw, *Sacred and Profane Beauty· The Holy in Art*, translated by D.E. Green, Holt, Rinehart & Winston, 1963, p 305.

4 See the quotation from Jung which forms the heading of Chapter 2.

5 C.G. Jung, op. cit vol. XVI, 1966, para 224

6 Ibid., para 289.

2 THEIRS BY RITE

1 C.G Jung, *The Collected Works*, vol. VIII, Routledge & Kegan Paul, 1969, para. 275

2 Victor Turner, *The Forest of Symbols*, Cornell University Press, 1970, p.102.

3 C.G. Jung, op. cit., vol. XVIII, para 616.

4 Monica Wilson, 'Nyakyusa Ritual in Symbolism', *American Anthropological Review*, vol. XXXVI, no 2, 1954, p.231.

5 C.G. Jung, op. cit., vol. XVI, para. 176.

6   C G Jung, op cit , vol. XVIII, para 617
7   Henry Corbin, 'The Eternal Sophia', translated and edited by Molly Tuby, *Harvest*, no.31, 1985, p 9
8   Ibid , p.19.
9   C G. Jung, op cit., vol. XIV, para 743.
10 See Chapter 4. The reader is also referred to Chapter 5 for a more psychological explication of this process
11 James Hillman, 'Initiation as a transformation of consciousness about life involves necessarily a transformation of consciousness about sexuality', *The Myth of Analysis Three Essays in Archetypal Psychology*, Harper & Row, 1972, p.63
12 James Hillman, *Healing Fiction*, Station Hill Press, 1983, p 61
13 Father Thomas Carroll, 'The Church Virgin and Mother', *Images of the Untouched*, edited by Joanne Stroud and Gail Thomas, Spring Publications, 1982, p 108
14 Victor Turner, *The Ritual Process· Structure and Anti-Structure*, Cornell University Press, 1969, p 103

3   GROWING A WOMAN

1   Penelope Shuttle and Peter Redgrove, *The Wise Wound. Menstruation and Everywoman*, Victor Gollancz, 1978, p.274
2   Bruce Lincoln, *Emerging from the Chrysalis: Studies in Rituals of Women's Initiation*, Harvard University Press, 1981.
3   Ibid , p 63 ff and p 93
4   Ibid.
5   C G. Jung, *The Collected Works*, vol. VI, Routledge & Kegan Paul, 1971 'Definitions', 49, Soul-Image (Anima/Animus), para. 808 forward; Emma Jung, *Animus and Anima*, Spring Publications, 1969; Andrew Samuels, Bani Shorter and Fred Plaut, *A Critical Dictionary of Jungian Analysis*, Routledge & Kegan Paul, 1986.
6   Jung, Emma, p.33
7   Mircea Eliade, *Myths, Dreams and Mysteries*, Collins, 1974, p 221
8   C.G Jung, *Memories, Dreams, Reflections*, recorded and edited by Aniela Jaffe, translated from the German by Richard and Clara Winston, Pantheon Books, 1963, p.109.
9   C G Jung, op. cit , vol XVI, para 185

10 Shuttle and Redgrove, p 90, as well as other references

11 John Beebe, MD, 'The Father's Anima', *The Father*, Contemporary Jungian Perspectives, edited and with an introduction by Andrew Samuels, Free Association Books, 1985

12 Mircea Eliade, *The Myth of the Eternal Return or, Cosmos and History*, Princeton University Press, 1974, p 18.

4 LOST VIRGINITY

1 Joseph F Rychlak, 'Jung as Dialectician and Teleologicist', *Jung in Modern Perspective*, edited by Renos K Papadopoulos and Graham S Saayman, Wildwood House, p.51

2 Carl Kerényi, *Eleusis Archetypal Image of Mother and Daughter*, translated from the German by Ralph Manheim, Pantheon Books, 1967, for a full description and hermeneutical essay on the mystery rites.

3 John Layard, *The Virgin Archetype*, Spring Publications, 1977, p 289

4 Kerényi, p.147.

5 C G Jung, *The Collected Works*, vol. VIII, Routledge & Kegan Paul, 1969, para. 618

6 Metropolitan Anthony, 'Body and Matter in Spiritual Life', *Sacrament and Image· Essays in the Christian Understanding of Men*, edited by A N Allchin, The Fellowship of St Alban and St Sergius, 1967, p.36.

7 Philip Sherrard, *Christianity and Eros· Essays on the Theme of Sexual Love*, SPCK, 1976, p.41.

8 Henry Corbin, 'The Eternal Sophia', translated and edited by Molly Tuby, *Harvest* no 31, 1985, p.19.

9 Ibid., p.11, '.   an open attitude to the irrational is not to be equated with abdication to the absurd '

10 Bruce Lincoln, *Emerging from the Chrysalis· Studies in Rituals of Women's Initiation*, Harvard University Press, 1981, p 81

11 Mircea Eliade, *Images and Symbols· Studies in Religious Symbolism*, translated by Philip Mairet, Sheed & Ward, 1969, Chapter entitled 'Symbolism of the "Centre" ', esp. p.39.

12 Layard, p.307.

13 Andrew Samuels, Bani Shorter, Fred Plaut, *A Critical Diction-*

ary of Jungian Analysis, Routledge & Kegan Paul, 1986, entry on *incest*.

14 C G. Jung, op. cit., vol V, para. 415

15 Lincoln, p.85.

16 Kerényi, p.141.

17 Ibid, p 147.

18 Ibid, p.101.

19 Mother C.E Putnam, 'The Image as Sacramental', *Sacrament and Image: Essays in the Christian Understanding of Man*, edited by A M Allchin, Fellowship of St Alban and St Sergius, 1967, p.15.

5 ENDANGERED DAUGHTER

1 C.G Jung, *The Collected Works*, vol. XVIII, Routledge & Kegan Paul, 1977, para. 1507.

2 C. Kerényi, *Eleusis· Archetypal Image of Mother and Daughter*, translated from the German by Ralph Manheim, Pantheon Books, 1967, p.169

3 Mircea Eliade, *Myths, Dreams and Mysteries: The Encounter Between Contemporary Faiths and Archaic Reality*, translated by Philip Mairet, Collins, 1974, p.27

4 Nathan Schwartz-Salant, *Narcissism and Character Transformation The Psychology of Narcissistic Character Disorders*, Inner City Books, 1980, ch.1, Part 2, 'Profile of the Narcissistic Character', p.37 forward.

5 Dr Kathrin Asper, *Depression, Dark Night of the Soul*, Guild Lecture No 222, The Guild of Pastoral Psychology, 1986.

6 Marija Gimbutas, *The Gods and Goddesses of Old Europe, 7000–3500 BC*, Thames & Hudson, 1974, p.199

7 James Hillman, *Loose Ends· Primary Papers on Archetypal Psychology*, Spring Publications, 1975, p.67.

8 C.G. Jung, op cit., vol. IX, Part ii, para. 42.

9 Robert Stein, *Incest and Human Love*, The Betrayal of the Soul in Psychotherapy, Penguin Books Inc 1974, p.43.

10 For further discussion of this theme see paper on projective identification, Nathan Schwartz-Salant, Proceedings of the Twelfth Congress, International Association for Analytical

Psychology, Daimon Verlag, forthcoming.

11 Philip Sherrard, *Christianity and Eros: Essays on the Theme of Sexual Love*, SPCK, 1976, p.14

12 See note 1

13 James Hillman, *The Myth of Analysis Three Essays in Archetypal Psychology*, Harper & Row, 1972, p 15.

14 Sherrard, p 57.

15 Victor Turner, *The Ritual Process. Structure and Anti-Structure*, Cornell University Press, 1979, p.106

6 . . . AND EVER VIRGIN

1 John Layard, *The Virgin Archetype*, Spring Publications, 1977, p 257.

2 Ibid., p 257f. The quotations are made from the English translation by William Watkins. *Of Conversion, a sermon to the clergy by Saint Bernard of Clairvaux*, translated by William Watkins, London, 1938

3 C.G Jung, *The Collected Works*, vol. VI, Routledge & Kegan Paul, 1971, para. 789f as well as Andrew Samuels, Bani Shorter and Dr Alfred Plaut, *A Critical Dictionary of Jungian Psychology*, Routledge & Kegan Paul, 1986, the entry on the *self.*

4 Layard, p 306

5 Henry Corbin, 'The Eternal Sophia', translated and edited by Molly Tuby, *Harvest*, no.31, 1985, p 19

6 C.G. Jung, vol. IX, op. cit , Part ii, para. 321. See also Jung, vol XVI, op. cit. paras 525 and 531.

7 St Maximos the Confessor, 'First Century on Theology', *The Philokalia*, vol II, translated from the Greek and edited by G E.H Palmer, Philip Sherrard, Kallistos Ware, Faber & Faber, 1981, p.128.

8 Victor Turner, *The Ritual Process· Structure and Anti-Structure*, Cornell University Press, 1977, p.103

9 Ibid.

10 Vladimir Lossky, 'Panagia', *In the Image and Likeness of God*, Mowbrays, 1975, p 199

11 For the connectedness between theology and a woman's

personal psychology see Ann Belford Ulanov, *Receiving Woman Studies in the Psychology and Theology of the Feminine*, The Westminster Press, 1981

12   C.G. Jung, op. cit , vol XI, para. 757

13   Ibid, para 838

14   Mother C E Putnam, 'The Image as Sacramental', *Sacrament and Image· Essays in the Christian Understanding of Man*, edited by A.M. Allchin, Fellowship of St Albans and St Sergius, 1967, p 15.

15   Marina Warner, 'The Immaculate Conception', *Alone of All Her Sex· The Myth and Cult of the Virgin Mary*, Pan Books, 1985, p.236f

16   C.G. Jung, op. cit , vol. XI para 400

17   St Augustine, Commentary on Psalm 147. Quoted in Paul Evdokimov, *The Sacrament of Love*, translated by Anthony Gythiel and Victoria Steadman, St Vladimir's Seminary Press, 1985, p.170.

18   James Hillman, *The Myth of Analysis Three Essays in Archetypal Psychology*, Harper & Row, 1978, p 91

19   Ibid.

20   For amplifications from two widely divergent sources see St Maximos the Confessor, p.170 and Adolf Guggenbuhl-Craig, *Marriage Dead or Alive*, translated by Murray Stein, Spring Publications, 1977, p 29.

21   Layard, op cit , p.342.

22   Philip Sherrard, *Christianity and Eros Essays on the Theme of Sexual Love*, SPCK, 1976, p.64.

23   Ibid., p 65

24   C G Jung, op. cit., vol XI, paras 123, 748 and 755.

25   James Hillman, 'Salt: A Chapter in Alchemical Psychology', *Images of the Untouched. Virginity in Psyche, Myth and Community*, edited by Joanne Stroud and Gail Thomas, Spring Publications, 1982, p 113.

SUGGESTIONS FOR FURTHER READING

Argüelles, Miriam and José, *The Feminine*, Shambala

Begg, Ean, *The Cult of the Black Virgin*, Routledge & Kegan Paul

Boen, Jean Shinoda, *Goddesses in Every Woman. New Psychology of the Feminine*, Harper & Row.

Buhrmann, M. Vera, *Living in Two Worlds. Communication between a White Healer and Her Black Counterparts*, Chiron.

D'Alviella, Goblet, *The Mysteries of Eleusis: The Secret Rites and Rituals of the Classical Greek Mystery Tradition*, Aquarian Press.

De Castillejo, Irene Claremont, *Knowing Woman· A Feminine Psychology*, Putnams

Downing, Christine, *The Goddess*, Crossroad Publishing.

Eliade, Mircea, *Rites and Symbols of Initiation*, Harper & Row.

Eliade, Mircea, *Myths, Dreams and Mysteries. The Encounter Between Contemporary Faiths and Archaic Reality*, Collins

Englesman, Joan Chamberlain, *The Feminine Dimension of the Divine*, The Westminster Press.

Hall, Nor, *The Moon and the Virgin· Reflections on the Archetypal Feminine*, Harper & Row

Harding, M. Esther, *Woman's Mysteries· Ancient and Modern*, Harper & Row

Henderson, Joseph, *Thresholds of Initiation*, Wesleyan.

Hillman, James, *Myth of Analysis Three Essays in Archetypal Psychology*, Harper & Row.

Jacoby, Mario, *The Analytic Encounter· Transference and Human Relationship*, Inner City Books.

Jung, C.G and Kerényi, Carl, *Introduction to a Science of Mythology: The Myth of the Divine Child and the Mysteries of Eleusis*, Routledge & Kegan Paul

Jung, Emma, *Animus and Anima*, Spring Publications

Kerényi, C., *Eleusis· Archetypal Image of Mother and Daughter*, Pantheon.

Kupfermann, Jeanette, *The MsTaken Body*, Granada.

Larsen, Stephen, *The Shaman's Doorway Opening the Mythic Imagination to Contemporary Consciousness*, Harper & Row.

Layard, John, *The Virgin Archetype*, Spring Publications.

Lincoln, Bruce, *Emerging from the Chrysalis: Studies in the Rituals of Women's Initiation*, Harvard.

Owen, Ursula, *Fathers: Reflections by Daughters*, Virago

Perera, Sylvia Brinton, *Descent to the Goddess*, Inner City Books

Pratt, Annis, *Archetypal Patterns in Women's Fiction*, Harvester Press.

Samuels, Andrew, ed. *The Father· Contemporary Jungian Perspectives*, Free Association (includes 'The Concealed Body Language of Anorexia Nervosa' by Bani Shorter).

Shostak, Marjorie, *Nisa The Life and Words of a !Kung Woman*, Penguin

Shuttle, Penelope, and Redgrove, Peter, *The Wise Wound, Menstruation and Everywoman*, Gollancz.

Stroud, Joanne, and Thomas, Gail, eds, *Images of the Untouched· Virginity in Psyche, Myth and Community*, Spring Publications.

Stein, Robert, *Incest and Human Love. The Betrayal of the Soul in Psychotherapy*, Penguin.

Te Paske, Bradley, A., *Rape and Ritual A Psychological Study*, Inner City Books.

Turner, Victor, *The Ritual Process. Structure and Anti-Structure*, Cornell University Press

Ulanov, Ann Belford, *Receiving Woman*, Westminster

Ulanov, Ann Belford, *The Feminine*, North Western.

van Gennep, Arnold, *The Rites of Passage*, Routledge & Kegan Paul.

Vitale, Augusto, Stein, Murray, Hillman, James, Neumann, Erich, Von der Heydt, Vera, *Fathers and Mothers. Five Papers on the Archetypal Background of Family Psychology*, Spring Publications.

Warner, Marina, *Alone of all Her Sex: The Myth and Cult of the Virgin Mary*, Pan Books.

Washbourn, Penelope, *Becoming Woman· The Quest for Wholeness in Female Experience,* Harper & Row.

Wheelwright, Jane Hollister, *The Death of a Woman,* St Martin's Press.

Whitmont, Edward C , *Return of the Goddess Femininity, Aggression and the Modern Grail Quest,* Routledge & Kegan Paul.

Woodman, Marion, *Addiction to Perfection. The Still Unravished Bride,* Inner City Books.

INDEX

Source UK Ltd.
eynes UK
022330060223
9UK00001B/142